Matthew Arnold

Dover Beach

Edited by

Jonathan Middlebrook
San Francisco State College

The Merrill Literary Casebook Series
Edward P. J. Corbett, Editor

Charles E. Merrill Publishing Company
A Bell & Howell Company
Columbus, Ohio

For my colleagues

ISBN: 0-675-09336-8

Library of Congress Catalog Number: 79-113744

1 2 3 4 5 6 7 8 9 10 — 74 73 72 71 70

Printed in the United States of America

Foreword

The Charles E. Merrill Literary Casebook Series deals with short literary works, arbitrarily defined here as "works which can be easily read in a single sitting." Accordingly, the series will concentrate on poems, short stories, brief dramas, and literary essays. These casebooks are designed to be used in literature courses or in practical criticism courses where the instructor wants to expose his students to an extensive and intensive study of a single, short work or in composition courses where the instructor wants to expose his students to the discipline of writing a research paper on a literary text.

All of the casebooks in the series follow this format: (1) foreword; (2) the author's introduction; (3) the text of the literary work; (4) a number of critical articles on the literary work; (5) suggested topics for short papers on the literary work; (6) suggested topics for long (10-15 pages) papers on the literary work; (7) a selective bibliography of additional readings on the literary work; (8) general instructions for the writing of a research paper. Some of the casebooks, especially those dealing with poetry, may carry an additional section, which contains such features as variant versions of the work, a closely related literary work, comments by the author and his contemporaries on the work.

So that students might simulate first-hand research in library copies of books and bound periodicals, each of the critical articles carries full bibliographical information at the bottom of the first page of the article, and the text of the article carries the actual page-numbers of the original source. A notation like /131/ after a word in the text indicates that *after* that word in the original source the article went over to page 131. All of the text between that number and the next number, /132/, can be taken as occurring on page 131 of the original source.

Edward P.J. Corbett
General Editor

Contents

Introduction

Two Events of 1851

1 May–11 October: the Great Exhibition in London
c. 19–30 June: Matthew Arnold journeys "to Dover and Back"

For the Victorian middle-class, the major event of the year 1851 was the Great Exhibition, an enormous world's fair which proved what most middle-class Englishmen already believed: England was the richest, most industrially advanced nation in the world. The overall theme of the Great Exhibition was world-wide progress under the beneficent dictatorship of Queen Victoria and her councillors. The dominant or public spirit of the age is nowhere better rendered than in Thackeray's *May-Day Ode*, written to celebrate the opening of the Exhibition in its huge Crystal Palace, the most extraordinary piece of architecture produced in the age of iron and steam. Here are some excerpts from Thackeray's *Ode*:

> A quiet green but few days since
> With cattle browsing in the shade:
> And here are lines of bright arcade
>   In order raised!
> A palace as for a fairy prince,
> A rare pavilion, such as man
> Never saw since mankind began,
>   And built and glazed!

* * *

> Behold her in her Royal place;
> A gentle lady; and the hand
> That sways the sceptre of this land,
>   How frail and weak!
> Soft is the voice, and fair the face:
> She breathes amen to prayer and hymn;
> No wonder that her eyes are dim,
>   And pale her cheek.

1

This moment round her empire's shores
The winds of Austral winter sweep,
And thousands lie in midnight sleep
        At rest today.
Oh! awful is that crown of yours,
Queen of innumerable realms
Sitting beneath the budding elms
        Of English May!

* * *

From Mississippi and from Nile—
From Baltic, Ganges, Bosphorus,
In England's ark assembled thus
        Are friend and guest.
Look down the mighty sunlit aisle,
And see the sumptuous banquet set,
The brotherhood of nations met
        Around the feast!

* * *

Look yonder where the engines toil:
These England's arms of conquest are,
The trophies of her bloodless war:
        Brave weapons these.
Victorious over wave and soil,
With these she sails, she weaves, she tills,
Pierces the everlasting hills
        And spans the seas.

* * *

Swell, organ, swell your trumpet blast,
March, Queen and Royal pageant, march
By splendid aisle and springing arch
        Of this fair Hall
And see! above the fabric vest,
God's boundless heaven is bending blue,
God's peaceful sunlight's beaming through,
        And shines o'er all.

Thackeray's *Ode* is representative of what we should first think of when we define the epithet *Victorian*. For the word still is an epithet to us, suggesting this brash faith that progress, wealth, and peace are all fruits to be cultivated in God's sight in an English garden. And *Victorian* as an epithet of course also suggests the massive inhibitions and repressions of the last pre-Freudian age, the age when legs became limbs and Bowdler's cleaned-up versions of Shakespeare were the ones fit for public display.

Yet the enduring poetry of an age is seldom that which gains the most immediate public acceptance, so it is hardly surprising that the major English literary event of 1851 was not the *May-Day Ode*. It was, we now know, Matthew Arnold's "Dover Beach," a poem extraordinarily moving by itself, and one which should also lead us to the fuller meaning of the descriptive term, *Victorian*.

The characteristic note of the great Victorians like Carlyle, Dickens, Ruskin, and Arnold himself, is the note of opposition. They see the self-confidence and blind pride of unchecked industrial exploitation and are appalled. Their usual mode of response is satiric, whether in such magnificent grotesques as Dickens' Josiah Bounderby or in Arnold's own straight-forward denunciations: "we all call ourselves," he writes in *Culture and Anarchy*, "in the sublime and aspiring language of religion which I have before noticed, *children of God*. Children of God;—it is an immense pretension!—and how are we to justify it? By the works which we do, and the word which we speak. And the work which we collective children of God do, our grand centre of life, our *city* which we have builded for us to dwell in, is London! London, with its unutterable external hideousness, and with its internal canker of *publicè egestas, privatim opulentia . . .*" [poverty of public expenditure, private opulence].

But even if we add the assault the Victorians themselves made on their own dominant cultural values of undirected progress and unbridled wealth, we have not finished shifting *Victorian* from epithet to term unless we include a poem like "Dover Beach," a poem which makes no claim to public utterance, but which is Matthew Arnold's private meditation on the world which created the Great Exhibition. It is, quite simply, a world of despair, a world without faith and therefore dark, self-destructive, and producing only the vaguest possibility of human love. "Ah, love, let us be true / To one another . . ." —there is no guarantee in this poem of desolation that Arnold's prayer will be answered. With the addition of this sense of despair to the more familiar brashness and satire and sexual inhibition, our notion of what the term *Victorian* means is complete.

It is only hindsight which says that Matthew Arnold had to write "Dover Beach," but his family background certainly put him at the center of English public life at the same time that it made him less fit to participate wholeheartedly in it. Matthew Arnold was the oldest son of Thomas Arnold, one of the central men of his age. For many years, Matthew had to deal with the pressure of being known only as the son of illustrious Dr. Arnold, clergyman and Headmaster of Rugby School. Rugby is one of the English public (to Americans, private) schools, and Thomas Arnold changed the character of public-school education in England. His effect on public life in England is therefore practically immeasurable, for the public school was an essential part of English society. Patrick J. McCarthy describes the public school of that time in this fashion:

> It inculcated as natural, and therefore fixed, an attitude toward the class system. It accomplished this first by offering young men from all strata of the responsible classes—in addition to an education—their first meeting ground. It brought together the son of the rising city merchant looking for a suitable property in the country; the grandson of a cloth manufacturer and son of a baronet who trained the boy for Parliament by making him repeat the Sunday sermons; the earl's son, accustomed to being called "my lord" from birth and anxious to make a decent maiden speech before his peers; the clergyman's son, least favored of all these, but also least bound, except that his career must be proper to a gentleman. As a conservative force, operating below the level of consciousness, binding men together for life with the perdurable stuff of adolescent affection, and binding them to the society that produced them, the public school can hardly be overestimated.[1]

What Thomas Arnold did was remake Rugby and public-school teaching in his own image. Before his advent, the public school was the place where young barbarians passed their time in hazing, manly sport, no study, and riots often requiring troops to put down. Under Thomas Arnold, Rugby became a place of moral dedication and hard work. As McCarthy says,

> [Thomas Arnold] based perhaps his most important concept on an analogy between the history of states and man's upward struggle for individual salvation. In his eyes both are born in the darkness of paganism and sin; in youth both make their way by force and cunning; only mature persons and states can recognize moral law for what it is and choose for themselves the ways of justice and virtue. To choose correctly is not easy and involves a struggle with man's indolent, selfish, and corrupt nature. But to give in to that nature, to prefer what is to what can be, is to lose the battle to evil and deny Christianity.[2]

Matthew Arnold himself attended Rugby while his father was Headmaster, and the way was obviously open to him to move into any

---

[1] Patrick J. McCarthy, *Matthew Arnold and the Three Classes* (New York, 1964), pp. 3–4. Quoted by permission of Columbia University Press.
[2] McCarthy, pp. 12–13.

of the public careers England offered her chosen sons. He did, from time to time, make half-hearted attempts at political office. Yet the history of his early career is one of self-division and concealment of spiritual *malaise*. Generally, he presented to the world a cultivated foppishness and *insouciance*: while in the sixth form (a senior) at Rugby, he would parody his awesome father, making faces behind his back for the entertainment of the other scholars; at Oxford, he affected the French style, memorizing Béranger's *chansons* and letting his hair grow; worse still for a Rugby man named Arnold, he did not graduate from Oxford with highest honors, taking only a second-class degree in 1845. This obvious pattern of rejecting his father seems clear enough to a post-Freudian age, but Matthew Arnold had no psychiatrist to ease his confusion.

So outwardly, he maintained the pose of dandy, the opposite of all Rugby and Thomas Arnold expected of him. In 1846, he took the English young man's mandatory Parisian tour and decorously pursued an actress through the season. But privately, Matthew Arnold was exploring the spiritual wasteland, the void left by his rejection, not just of his father's authority over him, but of his father's beliefs as well.

What if Thomas Arnold's sense of the immediate Christian significance of life's battle no longer answered to the next generation's needs? (Long after his father's death, Matthew wrote to his mother that Thomas Arnold was the last clergyman who could unhypocritically hold office in the Church of England.) Matthew found himself adrift in a newly hostile century. If God were no longer an immanent force in nature, if His presence were no longer felt in the pulse of human life, then man was left alone with nature as the 19th century was discovering it in the age of Darwin: mechanistic, relentless, indifferent to individual life and moral sensitivities.

Matthew Arnold took to writing poetry. He did not write very much, and a lot of what he did write is not very good. He published his first, thin volume in 1849 and had finished his major work by 1853. The spirit of this major work is defeat, sorrow, and one other thing, honesty. Faced with the bourgeois insensitivity of the Great Exhibition and what he felt to be the political blindness of the English upper classes, Matthew Arnold spoke privately in his poetry of the hollowness of the great English dream of a triumphant Christian march to Heaven. If the public utterance of the 19th century was "Onward Christian soldiers, marching as to war," the private knowledge of a man acquainted and educated with the leaders was "We are here, as on a darkling plain . . ./ Where ignorant armies clash by night."

It is unfair to Arnold to leave his portrait drawn in such shades of melancholy. "Dover Beach" is the most widely anthologized poem in English, but Arnold wrote it when he was under thirty, and as our sense of the term *Victorian* suggests, there is more to Arnold and the 19th-century English literature than this one poem. Arnold himself could no more rest content with the despair of the poem than he could bring himself to believe that the Great Exhibition was itself a significant advance toward the kingdom of God. What he did was cast his lot with the opposition: he became one of the great critics and satirists of his age. The dandaical part of him turned out to have a cutting and brilliant wit. Here, in "The Function of Criticism at the Present Time," Arnold takes on a particularly egregious piece of English self-satisfaction:

> "A shocking child murder has just been committed at Nottingham. A girl named Wragg left the workhouse there on Saturday morning with her young illegitimate child. The child was soon afterwards found dead on Mapperly Hills, having been strangled. Wragg is in custody."
>
> Nothing but that; but, in juxtaposition with the absolute eulogies of Sir Charles Adderley and Mr. Roebuck, how eloquent, how suggestive are those few lines! "Our old Anglo-Saxon breed, the best in the whole world!"—how much that is harsh and ill-favoured there is in this best! *Wragg!* If we are to talk of ideal perfection, of "the best in the whole world," has anyone reflected what a touch of grossness in our race, what an original short-coming in the more delicate spiritual perceptions, is shown by the natural growth among us of such hideous names,—Higgin-bottom, Stiggins, Bugg! In Ionia and Attica they were luckier in this respect than "the best race in the world"; by the Ilissus there was no Wragg, poor thing! And "our unrivalled happiness";—what an element of grimness, bareness, and hideousness mixes with it and blurs it; the workhouse, the dismal Mapperly Hills,—how dismal those who have seen them will remember;—the gloom, the smoke, the cold, the strangled illegitimate child! "I ask you whether, the world over or in past history, there is anything like it?" Perhaps not, one is inclined to answer; but at any rate, in that case, the world is [not] very much to be pitied. And the final touch,—short, bleak and inhuman: *Wragg is in custody.* The sex lost in the confusion of our unrivalled happiness: or (shall I say?) the superfluous Christian name lopped off by the straightforward vigour of our old Anglo-Saxon breed! There is profit for the spirit in such contrasts as this; criticism serves the cause of perfection by establishing them.

Matthew Arnold made himself master of the infuriating and fastidious insult woven around the grimmest of Victorian social truths: the concomitant of middle-class wealth was the creation of the most ghastly slums and conditions the world had yet imagined possible, or impossible, for that matter. Arnold's is a particularly English mode of piercing the tough rind of complacency and making the middle-class Englishman acknowledge the doubts within. His mode combines the unquestioned right of a public school and Oxford man to sneer at a merely wealthy man with the genuine horror, which of course was felt by the middle-class itself, at the awful conditions of the English poor.

Arnold's satiric mode is also perfect because it answered both to his audience, who were Victorians in the full sense of the term as we've discussed it, and because it answered to his own experience of public dandyism and private disillusion. For the best of Arnold's essays have both the elegant, somewhat priggish flyting of the Wragg passage and a central sadness very much like that of "Dover Beach." Here is the conclusion of "The Function of Criticism." He is judging his own century and finds it wanting in the highest creative power, the power to make great literature: "The epochs of Aeschylus and Shakespeare make us feel their pre-eminence. In an epoch like those is, no doubt, the true life of literature; there is the promised land, toward which criticism can only beckon. That promised land it will not be ours to enter, and we shall die in the wilderness: but to have desired to enter it, to have saluted it from afar, is already, perhaps, the best distinction among contemporaries; it will certainly be the best title to esteem with posterity." Arnold as Moses, the man who can only see, not enter, the Promised Land! There is at once presumption and humility in the analogy: presumption, that he should liken himself to the leader of a chosen people; humility, that for him the analogy speaks to his sense that others will be able to do what he himself cannot. Together, the presumption and humility blend into the mature self-knowledge of the man who, when young, wrote "Dover Beach." Seen from the perspective of Arnold's whole career, the poem becomes less of a claim that all modern civilization is hollow and more of a challenge to recognize that awful possibility, to feel it in the convincing way "Dover Beach" makes us feel it, and then to go on to wrest joy from life anyway.

Arnold himself does not appear to have achieved more than honest contentment. All of his brilliant essays are framed by a dark despair which raises them above persiflage and makes them the literature of a man dealing with the most modern sense of cosmic loneliness. Which modern authors do more?

Dover Beach

The sea is calm to-night.
The tide is full, the moon lies fair
Upon the straits;—on the French coast the light
Gleams and is gone; the cliffs of England stand,
Glimmering and vast, out in the tranquil bay.
Come to the window, sweet is the night-air!
Only, from the long line of spray
Where the sea meets the moon-blanch'd land,
Listen! you hear the grating roar
Of pebbles which the waves draw back, and fling,
At their return, up the high strand,
Begin, and cease, and then again begin,
With tremulous cadence slow, and bring
The eternal note of sadness in.

Sophocles long ago
Heard it on the Ægæan, and it brought
Into his mind the turbid ebb and flow
Of human misery; we
Find also in the sound a thought,
Hearing it by this distant northern sea.

The Sea of Faith
Was once, too, at the full, and round earth's shore
Lay like the folds of a bright girdle furl'd.
But now I only hear
Its melancholy, long, withdrawing roar,
Retreating, to the breath
Of the night-wind, down the vast edges drear
And naked shingles of the world.

Ah, love, let us be true
To one another! for the world, which seems

This is the text of the 1890 MacMillan and Co., Ltd., edition, the last edition
Arnold himself prepared for the press.

To lie before us like a land of dreams,
So various, so beautiful, so new,
Hath really neither joy, nor love, nor light,
Nor certitude, nor peace, nor help for pain;
And we are here as on a darkling plain
Swept with confused alarms of struggle and flight,
Where ignorant armies clash by night.

Lionel Trilling

Commentary*

Matthew Arnold occupies a rather strange place in the community of English poets. Few people, I think, would include him among the great poets of England. The body of his work is not large, certainly not in comparison with the production of other poets of the Victorian age, and of this relatively small canon only a handful of poems are wholly successful. Yet Arnold is generally ranked as one of the three most important poets of his time, the other two being Tennyson and Browning. Indeed, despite his manifest faults, Arnold as a poet makes an appeal to the reader of today which is likely to be greater than that of either of his two imposing contemporaries.

A phrase I have just used, "Arnold as a poet," will perhaps seem odd and need explanation. We do not speak of "Tennyson *as* a poet" or of "Browning *as* a poet"—they *were* poets, we know them as nothing else. But Arnold, having begun his literary life in poetry, gave up what we might call the professional practice of the art at about the age of thirty. It was not possible for him to make an adequate living by writing alone and he therefore accepted an appointment as an inspector of elementary schools; he served in this capacity until a few years before his death. The work was fatiguing and depressing, and he could command neither the leisure nor the emotional energy that poetry requires. He did, however, find it possible to write prose, and, working in that medium, he became one of the leading intellectual figures of England. He was the most admired literary critic of his day, and, indeed, is generally accounted one of the great critics of the world. He was a very notable theorist of politics, and his writings on religion played an important part in the crisis of faith which so deeply distressed many of his con-

* Reprinted from *The Experience of Literature:* A Reader With Commentaries by Lionel Trilling. New York: Holt, Rinehart, and Winston, 1967, pp. 899–901, by permission of the publisher. Copyright © 1967 by Lionel Trilling.

temporaries. Perhaps more than any other man of his time and nation
he perceived the changes that were taking place in the conditions of
life and in the minds of men to bring into being the world we now
know—in certain respects he was, of all the intellectual figures of his
period, the most modern.

The sensitivity to the cultural circumstances of his day which Arnold
showed in his prose does much to explain his interest as a poet. Both
in his early poems, which make up the larger body of his canon, and
in the infrequent later poems, some of which are among his best,
Arnold showed an awareness of the emotional conditions of modern life
which far exceeds that of any other poet of his time. He spoke with
great explicitness and directness of the alienation, isolation, and excess
of consciousness leading to doubt which are, as so much of /900/ later
literature testifies, the lot of modern man. And it is plain that he speaks
from an unabashedly personal experience of pain, fatigue, and thwarted
hope—his poetry has for us the authority of authenticity even when it
lacks a high poetic grace.

"Dover Beach," however, can scarcely be said to be lacking in grace.
It is one of the handful of Arnold's wholly successful poems and among
these it is pre-eminent. For many readers it is the single most memorable poem of the Victorian age. In it the authenticity that is in general
the characteristic note of Arnold's poetry achieves a peculiar pathos.
The diction is perfect in its lightness and simplicity. The verse, moving
in a delicate crescendo of lyricism from the muted beginning to the
full-voiced desperate conclusion, is superbly managed. Not the least
of the elements of its success is that a poem so modest in tone and in
apparent scope should contain within it such magnificent vistas of
space and time.

The poem is dramatic in the sense that, although there is only one
speaker, there are two characters, the speaker and the woman he addresses as his love, presumably his wife. The setting of the dramatic
scene is of central importance; the American reader might not recognize what an English reader would know at once, that the couple are
staying at a hotel, for Dover is one of the two English ports from which
one takes ship to cross the English Channel to France. The circumstance that the couple are setting out on a journey abroad makes it all
the more likely that they should be inclined to think of the world as
being "so various, so beautiful, so new."

The window through which the speaker is gazing and to which he
invites his companion might well bring to mind the "magic casements"
of the [Keats's] "Ode to a Nightingale." Like the window in Keats's
poem, it opens "on the foam / Of perilous seas," and on forlorn lands,

although not faery lands. It has the effect of framing the view and of emphasizing the sense of vista that plays so material a part in the poem. The immediate view—the great white chalk cliffs of Dover, the French coast twenty miles off, indicated by the momentary light, the moonlit waters of the Channel between—is in itself sufficiently impressive. But it opens out both in space and time to reach across Europe to the Aegean Sea and ancient Greece. It is worth noting that several of Arnold's poems depend for their most moving effects upon similar representations of great vistas both of geography and history and that in one of his early sonnets Arnold refers to Europe as "The Wide Prospect," deriving the phrase from a possible translation of the Greek name, and seeming to suggest that it was the essential quality of the European mind that it could encompass great reaches of space and time. Although in general Arnold's distances imply liberation and even joy, in "Dover Beach," when the imagination goes beyond the Aegean, it proceeds in darkness to the "vast edges drear / And naked shingles of the world."

The emptiness and despair of the vision bring the speaker back to the place from which his imagination had started, to the room from whose window he looks out, and he turns in despairing sadness to his companion, at that moment seemingly the only other person in the world, to offer her, and ask from her, loyalty in love. Perhaps literature does not know a love avowal and a love plea so sad as these—perhaps never before in literature has a lover given a *reason* for love, and a reason which, while asserting its necessity, denies its delight. It is believed by all lovers that love has the power not only of making the world various and /901/ beautiful and new, but also of maintaining it in variety, beauty, and novelty. But the lover of "Dover Beach" denies love's efficacy in this respect. Of all that love may be presumed to give, he asks only loyalty in a world that promises neither joy nor peace.

It is to this pass that the lover has been brought by his sense of modern life, which has seen the ebbing of the sea of faith. We assume that he means religious faith, and this assumption is borne out by other of Arnold's poems in which the diminution of religious faith is a reason for melancholy. But Arnold felt that the lessening of religious faith went hand in hand with the lessening of personal energy, vitality, and confidence, of that happy, unquestioning attachment to life which William James called "animal faith." When Arnold speaks of Sophocles hearing the roar of the pebbles on the beach under the receding wave and of its having brought "into his mind the turbid ebb and flow / Of human misery," he is almost certainly making reference to the opening of the third chorus of Sophocles' *Antigone*. Here is the passage in the translation of R. J. Jebb: "Blest are they whose days have not tasted of evil. For when a house hath once been shaken from heaven, there the curse fails nevermore, passing from life to life of the race [i.e., family]; even as, when the surge is driven over the darkness of the deep by the fierce breath of Thracian sea-winds, it rolls up the black sand from the depths, and there is a sullen roar from the wind-vexed headlands that front the blows of the storm." The chorus ostensibly speaks of the misery of the members of certain families living under a curse, and not of "human misery" in general. But the generalization can of course be made, and we may readily believe that Arnold had in mind the contrast between the passage from the third chorus to which he refers and the more famous second chorus of *Antigone*, which begins "Wonders are many, and none is more wonderful than man," and goes on to sing with joy of man's triumphs. It is the faith in man and his destiny so proudly expressed by the second chorus that has ebbed, leaving the world to bleakness.

The great grim simile with which the poem ends has attracted much attention, and efforts have been made to find the inspiration for it in Arnold's reading. The likeliest possibility is the account of the battle of Epipolae given by Thucydides in his *History of the Peloponnesian War* (Book VII, Chapters 43–44); this guess is encouraged by the circumstance that Arnold's father, Thomas Arnold, had published a well-known edition of the *History*. A striking quality of the simile is its unexpectedness. Up to this point the lovers have looked out on a world of wind and water, quite empty of people; now the scene is a plain filled with armies in strife. The suddenness of the shift reinforces the violence of the dark image of deteriorated existence.

Murray Krieger

"Dover Beach" and the Tragic Sense of Eternal Recurrence*

What are the characteristics of Matthew Arnold's "Dover Beach" that have earned a place for the poem so far above that of those maligned Victorian works which critics commonly consign to our willful neglect? To what extent has it earned its exemption from the common charges they bring against many of its contemporaries?

It would seem clear enough that in "Dover Beach" Arnold brings along his usual equipment, or, I might better term it, his *impedimenta*. The usual techniques and the usual patterns of thought which infect much of his verse and render it unsuccessful are apparent at once. The surprise is that the joining of them in this poem proves as happy as it does. There is, first, the well-known Arnold melancholy: the man of little faith in a world of no faith, who still hopes to maintain the spiritual dignity which the world of no faith now seems to deny him. There is also the typical nineteenth-century didactic formula which Arnold rarely failed to use by allowing his "poetic" observer to extort symbolic instruction from a natural scene. Finally there is here as elsewhere the mixture, perhaps the strange confusion, between a poetic diction and a diction that is modern, almost prosaic.

Arnold's easy but uneven rhetoric of melancholy often leads these characteristics to fail as he compounds them, but here they succeed, and in a way that reaches beyond the limitations of Arnold's period and of his own poetic sensibility. "Dover Beach" bears and rewards contemplation from the vantage point of the modern, and yet ancient, concept of time which has stirred our consciousness through writers like Mann, Proust, Virginia Woolf, T. S. Eliot—a concept of time as

* An essay reprinted from *The Play and the Place of Criticism*, by Murray Krieger, pages 69–78. © The Johns Hopkins Press, 1967. An earlier version of the essay appeared in the University of Kansas City Review, XXIII (October, 1956), 73–79.

15

existential rather than as chronologically historical, as the flow of
Bergson's dynamics, as the eternal and yet never-existing present. This
awareness which we associate with our sophisticated contemporary
can be seen somehow to emerge from Arnold's /70/ highly Victorian
"Dover Beach." We must determine how it manages to do so, how
the very weaknesses that generally characterize Arnold's poetic imagination serve here to create this tragic and extremely modern vision.
It is a vision which Arnold achieves neither as a nineteenth-century
optimist nor as a vague and confused rebel of his period who turns
to an equally nineteenth-century pessimism and simple melancholy;
it is a vision which he achieves by transcending his period and fore-
seeing the intellectual crisis which we too often think of as peculiar
to our own century[1].

A cursory reading of the poem discloses that all the stanzas but the
second are built on a similar two-part structure and that each recalls
the ones which have gone before. The first section in each of these
stanzas deals with that which is promising, hopeful; the second undercuts the cheer allowed by the first section and replaces the illusory
optimism with a reality which is indeed barren, hopeless. In these
subdivisions of stanzas there is also a sharp contrast in tone between
the pleasant connotations of the first section of these stanzas and the
less happy ones of the second. In each of them, too, there is a contrast
between the appeal to the sense of sight in the first section and the
appeal to the sense of hearing in the second.

And yet, these three stanzas are not, of course, mere repetitions of
each other. Each marks a subsequent development of the image—the
conflict between the sea and the land. With each succeeding stanza
the sea takes on a further meaning. I said earlier that this, like most
of Arnold's poems, deals with a natural scene and the moral application of the meaning perceived within it: the vehicle of the metaphor
and then the tenor carefully stated for us. In this poem, however, the
development from the natural scene to the human levels into which
it opens is much more successfully handled than elsewhere in his
work. Each level grows into the succeeding one without losing the
basic natural ingredients which initiated the image.

We can see that the natural scene described in the first stanza is
value-laden from the beginning. It is clear that nature itself—or at
least nature as sensuously perceived—does have immediate signifi-

---

[1] This paragraph may seem to imply that Nietzsche, whose phrase I have bor-
rowed for my title and my theme, is a twenties-century mind. In the sense in
which Arnold is predominantly a nineteenth-century mind, Nietzsche may very
well appear rather to belong in our own century.

cance, and moral significance, so that when the development and application are made later, we do not feel them as unnatural. By the third stanza the sea has of course /71/ become the "Sea of Faith,"[2] but the human relevance of the sea-land imagery is justified by the transitional second stanza. In addition, the image is handled completely in the terms which characterize its natural use in the first stanza. The sea-land conflict is still with us, still the motivating force of the insight the poem offers. And in the last stanza the sea-land conflict exists in the present, but, for Arnold and for these lovers, representative here of humanity at large, the historical present. The aphoristic impressiveness of the final lines of the poem is again justified in terms of the initial image of the first stanza, which they here recall and bring to its final fruition. The archetypal image of the sea, of the tides, and of the action of these as the sea meets the land—all these have been merged with the destiny of that humanity to which they have meant so much throughout its mythopoetic history.

As nature has thus—if I may use the word—*naturally* merged with man, so, through the use of middle part of the poem, has history merged with the present, has the recurrence, of which the sea, the tides, the meeting of land and sea have always stood as symbols, merged with the ever-historical present. This is why the second stanza of the poem is excluded from the parallel development of the others. It is the stanza which makes the poem possible, which brings us to "the ebb and flow of *human* misery," and brings us to the past even as we remain in the present. The image and its archetypal quality are indispensable to the poem. For the tidal ebb and flow, retreat and advance, and the endless nature of these are precisely what is needed to give Arnold the sense of the eternal recurrence which characterizes the full meaning of the poem.

But now to examine some of these general comments in greater detail by looking at the poem more closely. The first eight lines give us the scene as it appeals immediately to the sight of the poet viewing it. It is a good scene, one which finds favor with the poet. The value of the scene is indicated by adjectives like "calm," "full," "fair,"

---

[2] The surface triteness of this phrase is typical of Arnold's frequent and stereotyped use of a metaphorical sea, as in the many variations on "the Sea of Life" which dot his poems. (See, for example, "To Marguerite," "Despondency," "Human Life," "Self-Dependence," "A Summer Night," and "The Buried Life.") His failure to exploit this image freshly or even to show an awareness of the need for doing so accounts in large part for his poetic weakness elsewhere. We shall see later that "Dover Beach" is distinguished by Arnold's ability here to make his usual conception come alive through his manipulation of the central image of the poem.

"tranquil," "sweet," "moon-blanched." There is a sense of satisfaction, of utter completeness /72/ about the scene. But of course it is the sea which gives the feeling of ultimate pleasure. In the two places in which the land is mentioned there is something a bit less steady in the impression. The light on the French coast is not, after all, a steady light, and as it gleams and is gone so the cliffs of England, which seem to stand so steadily, yet are glimmering even as they are vast. The land, then, provides the only inconstancy, indeed the only qualification of the perfection of the scene.

The word "only" in line 7 introduces the contrasting mood which will characterize the later portion of the stanza. But before this later portion is given to us, there is the remainder of line 7 and all of line 8, which serve as a reminder of the satisfying first portion of the stanza, although "only" has already been introduced as a transition—one which serves to awaken us to the more unhappy attitude that is to follow. And with the word "listen" at the beginning of line 9, we are to be shocked out of our happy lethargy even as the poet is shocked out of his. The sharp trochaic foot and the long caesura which follows re-enforce this emphasis. And with this word we are transferred from the visual world to the auditory world.

One might almost say that the poet, until this point remarking about the perfection of the scene, has been remarking rather casually —that is, after an almost random glance at it. But here he meets the scene more intimately. He does not merely glance but comes into closer rapport with the scene by lending the more contiguous sense, that of his hearing. He now pays close attention to the scene, and what he hears replaces what he has merely seen as a casual onlooker. What he discovers is far less satisfying, and yet it is more profound than his earlier reaction because he now begins to catch the undertones and overtones of the scene before him, which he before was content to witness superficially. And here the sea is used much as, for example, Conrad and Melville use it. Its superficial placidity, which beguiles its viewer, belies the perturbed nature, the "underground" quality, of its hidden depths. As the more intimate, more aware, and more concerned faculty of hearing is introduced, the turmoil of sea meeting land becomes sensible. The shift in tone from the earlier portion of the stanza is made obvious by Arnold's use of "grating roar" immediately after the appeal to the ear has been made.

One may see in the shift from the eye to the ear also another purpose. It is Arnold's way of moving us from the here and the now to the everywhere and always, from the specific immediacy of the present scene to the more universal application his image must have to serve the rest of the poem. /73/ What we *see* must be a particular scene which is unique and irreplaceable, while our hearing may be lulled by similarities to identify the sounds of other places and other times with those before us now.[3] No sight is completely like any other; sounds may be far more reminiscent and may thus allow us to fancy that we are in another time, in another country. Identity of sound may lead the imagination to an identity of occasion.[4] Then not only is the sense of sight inadequate to grasp the profound perplexities of the situation so that the more subtle sense of hearing must be invoked, but, unlike the sense of hearing, the sense of sight is also incapable of permitting us to break free of the relentless clutch of the present occasion to wander relaxedly up and down the immensities of time.

The "eternal note of sadness," then, caused by the endless battle without victory and without truce between sea and land; this note representing the give-and-take of the tide which symbolically echoes the basic rhythmic pattern of human physio-psychology—this eternal note of sadness, heard also by Sophocles, connects the past at once with the presentness of the past and connects also this rhythmic pattern with the humanity who has taught it to serve them and yet ironically, as the Greeks among others have shown us, has instead served it. Even in the first stanza we saw nature as animated by the human mind, as immediately meaningful in human terms. In the second stanza its human relevance is made explicit. The word "turbid" (line 17) effectively joins the natural sense of the image to its human application as it combines the meaning of "muddied" with that of "confused." As Sophocles serves to read man into the natural image of the first stanza, thus making him one with the natural world, so with the final word ("we") of line 18 the present is read into the past;[5] and the circle of /74/ the natural order, now including within its circumference the wheel of human destiny and man-made time, is closed.

---

[3] I am indebted to Michael W. Dunn, who first suggested to me that Arnold is here using the greater dependence of the sense of sight on a single time-and-place occurrence.

[4] One can see a similar conceit operating in Wordsworth's "To the Cuckoo" and Keats' "Ode to a Nightingale." In each of these works, too, the poet (who here cannot use his sense of sight since he is unable to see the bird) allows himself to fancy, because only the sound of the bird's song reaches his senses, that the bird itself is somehow immortal even while it has temporal existence, that it has sung in other times and in other places. The illusion fostered by this romantic operation of synecdoche could become a valuable poetic instrument in the hands of such writers as these. See pp. 120-21, below, for an extension of this discussion as it applies to these poems.

[5] The effecting of this union may be aided by what may seem to be something like an unusual internal rhyme between two neighboring vowels, between the last syllable of *misery* and *we*. (It would of course be difficult to maintain this as an internal rhyme if one admits that the last syllable of *misery* is probably unstressed.)

The third stanza, in a manner parallel to the first, breaks into two contrasting parts. The first three lines present the promise of the visual image, the last five the despair to the auditory. In the first portion, to the sense of fullness and perfection which was ours in the first lines of the poem is now added the illusion of protectiveness—hence the "girdle" image. Not only is the sea characterized by its complete and self-sufficient perfection, but, like the divine "One" of Plotinus, it must overflow its bounds to salve, indeed to anoint, the imperfect land. Thanks to the passage of Sophocles, the extension of the sea to the human problem and hence to the "Sea of Faith" is now literally as well as metaphorically justified, although the image must remain true to its earlier formulation. And it does. After the "but" (line 24), which here has the same qualifying function as the disappointed "only" in the first stanza, we are returned to the sense of hearing and to the struggle between land and sea which it first introduced. The inevitable cycle must continue and every resurgence be followed by the equally necessary retreat. The advance we have made from the sea to the sea of faith and the added quality of protectiveness given by the "girdle" image bestow a new dimension to the hopelessness of the "naked shingles of the world," the words which close the stanza.

While the first line and a half of the last stanza, in which the poet addresses his beloved, may seem digressive, although they are prepared for in line 6 of the first stanza, they are involved in the development of the poem by the crucial adjective "true," which here means "faithful": the poet is posing the only and the hardly satisfying alternative—the personal alternative of mutual fidelity—for our abandonment by the sea of faith. And again there follows the antithesis between the vision which yields the Apollonian attitude and the cacophony of Dionysian turmoil. Here, however, the balance is swung more heavily than before in the direction of despair. For, we are told explicitly, the world of perfection now merely "seems" (line 30); the world of chaos exists "really" (line 33). The final image of battle, though far-grown from the land-sea conflict of the latter lines of the first stanza, is thoroughly consistent with it and can take its meaning only in terms of it. We are returned in effect to the pre-human natural world of the first stanza and to its primitivism as the clashing armies are finally characterized by the poet as "ignorant." The clash is endless, as endless as time and tide, and, viewed without faith, in terms of nothingness, is as purposeless. /75/ Man himself has now drawn his circle closed or rather has acknowledged the closedness of nature's circle—perhaps the same thing—and has joined with an ungrounded nature to assert his ignorance, his irresponsibility, his doom. But the doom man carries with him he carries only to assert with it his eternal recurrence, even if that which recurs does so but to be doomed again. For paradoxically, doom too is eternally recurrent.

We are, then, worse than returned to what I called a moment ago the pre-human natural world of the first stanza and its primitivism. For the "nature" of the first stanza, being, as we have seen, value-laden, existing only in terms of human perception, was indeed a nature that was humanized. It was seen as meaningful, indeed as purposive. The telic quality of the human was read into nature and, by animating it, made it also telic. But in the primitivism of the *"ignorant* armies" humanity is seen as atelic. The relationship has been reversed as the non-purposive quality of the nature of modern science has been read into man. As nature was humanized at the start, so here man is naturalized and, thus, deprived of his purposiveness, deadened. He has indeed become part of nature and hence, in the words of Keats, "become a sod." The poet, of course, rises above this death-in-life by his dedication to the personal, the I-and-Thou, relationship to his beloved, now that any more inclusive relationships have been shut off from him. But, more important, the poet's assertion of his still-lingering humanity consists primarily in his insistence on realizing fully the sense of its loss, in his refusal to be "ignorant" of it.

The poem may seem at first, despite some sideroads, to have a unilinear chronological development. After the natural scene of the present is given us in the first stanza, the word "eternal" in the last line of this stanza permits the poet to move back to Sophocles. Then, after briefly returning to the present in the latter part of the second stanza, the poet moves us back again in time, but now to the Christian Middle Ages.[6] With the introduction of the modern world and its skepticism in the latter part of the third stanza, the poet has prepared us to return to the present dramatic scene of the last stanza. But whatever sense of chronology this arrangement allows us is seen to be purely illusory because of the return in the final image of the poem to the primitivism and everlastingness of the image of tidal conflict with which we began. Similarly, in the very close parallelism of structure of the first, /76/ third, and concluding stanzas we feel the unprogressiveness of man's ever-repetitive circular history.

---

[6] Here we see Arnold managing to return to one of the favorite laments of so much of his prose as well as his verse: the irreplaceable psychological efficacy of the Christian medieval unity which, unfortunately, had to turn out to be so scientifically erroneous, and thus to him unacceptable, in its theological foundations.

The handling of the metrics and rhyme scheme reflect the other elements we have observed in the poem. The inexorable quality of the unending struggle as it is felt in such passages as

> . . . *the grating roar*
> *Of pebbles which the waves draw back, and fling,*
> *At their return, up the high strand,*
> *Begin, and cease, and then again begin* . . .

is obvious enough. But perhaps more significant is the development of the patterns of line-length and rhyme, which begin as relatively undefined and conclude as firm and under full control. Through the first three stanzas the intermixture of pentameter lines with shorter ones is unpredictable, and, similarly, there is no determinate rhyme scheme. While the poem clearly is written in rhyme, the echoes of the final syllables of the lines surprise us since there is no pattern which enables us to foresee when the sounds will recur. And yet they continually do recur in this seemingly undetermined way. Only the final word of line 9 ("roar") seems not to have any rhyme in its stanza; and even this may be claimed to be an off-rhyme with "fair" (line 2) and "air" (line 6), functioning to set up a tension between this line and the earlier pleasant portion of the stanza—precisely what we should expect of the noun which is characterized as "grating."

Thus until the last stanza is reached, the patternless rhymes suggest a continual recurrence, but one on which human meaning and form have not yet been bestowed. The echoes multiply, but they have not yet been cast into a significant mold. In the final stanza a clear rhyme scheme at last emerges (*abbacddcc*), and, further, for the first time the line-lengths even out. Between the initial trimeter and the concluding tetrameter are seven consistently pentameter lines. The problem of the poem, while certainly not resolved (poems rarely resolve problems, or ought to), has at least emerged as fully comprehensible, in terms of the poem at least. The meaning of the recurrence has become tragically and profoundly clear.

It may—and perhaps with some justice—be claimed that, if my prosodic analysis is valid, this manipulation of line-length and rhyme is, after all, a not very cunning trick, indeed is a highly mechanical contrivance. Or the poet's attempt to make the technical elements so obviously expressive may be charged and booked under Yvor Winters' "fallacy of imitative form." I shall skirt these issues since my purpose here is primarily explicative. In /77/ terms of this purpose it is enough to say that the versification, like the structure, the diction, and the archetypal imagery, marks out the repetitive inclusiveness of the human condition and its purposeless gyrations. The poem's form thus comes to be a commentary on the problem that is being poetically explored, a mirror which allows the poem to come to terms with itself.

But if the form helps indicate the price of eternal recurrence for a world robbed of its faith—the fate of being pitilessly bound by the inescapable circle—in the regularity it finally achieves, it indicates, too, the sole possibility for victory over the circle and freedom from it: the more than natural, the felt human awareness of its existence and its meaning. The tragic is at least an attainment, an attainment through the painful process of utter realization, realization of self, of nature, and of history. And the contemporaneity of the Western tradition in the poem is Arnold's way of proving that he has realized *it* and himself as its child.

Paull F. Baum

"Dover Beach"*

'Dover Beach', one of Arnold's most admired poems, was probably composed in the summer of 1851 and subsequently revised for the volume of *New Poems* in 1867. The evidences for this date are tenuous, but taken together amount to reasonable probability. 'Dover Beach' has something in common with 'Philomela,' which was published in 1853: a pleasing melancholy (Arnold's phrase for 'The Scholar-Gipsy'), a similar structure (the setting, with moonlight, the story, the personal appeal to Eugenia), a contrast of the present and the Greek background, and somewhat of the same metrical form.[1] It has even more in common with 'Stanzas from the Grande Chartreuse,' which was begun in the autumn of 1851 and published in *Fraser's* for April 1855. The similarity here is the contrast between the Greek and a modern in their loss of faith. Either poem might have suggested the other in the comparable parts, but it is more likely that Arnold used the same idea in both at about the same time. (Bonnerot, pp. 369–71, has emphasized the parallels.) /86/

Nearly everyone assumes that 'Dover Beach' was written with Mrs. Arnold in mind; Tinker and Lowry are distinguished exceptions. In the 1867 volume it immediately followed 'Calais Sands' (though it was immediately followed by the Marguerite poem, 'The Terrace at

* Reprinted from *Ten Studies of the Poetry of Matthew Arnold*. Durham: Duke University Press, 1958, pp. 85–96, by permission of the publisher.

[1] Eugenia appears first in 'Horatian Echo,' written in 1847, and again in 'Philomela,' which was written on the fly-leaf of a copy of Latham's *English Language*, London, 1848. Tinker and Lowry speak of her as "the poet's imaginary mistress" and as "probably a lay figure, like the lady addressed in the last paragraph of 'Dover Beach'" (*Commentary*, pp. 59, 164, 165, 59). In other words, nothing is known about her.

24

Berne') and Sir E. K. Chambers says plainly *"Dover Beach* and *Calais Sands* are both related to *Faded Leaves."*[2] If one assumes further that the picture of Dover Beach in the moonlight—"Come to the window" —represents the stop of Arnold and his wife at Dover on their wedding journey in June 1851, there would be corroboration in the later lines

> *the world which seems*
> *To lie before us . . .*
> *So various, so beautiful, so new;*

and there would be additional poignancy in the appeal "let us be true To one another" in spite of all its hostile forces.

I

The poem consists of four sections or stanzas: the setting (1–14) ; Sophocles, or the Greek parallel (15–20) ; the sea at Dover and the Sea of Faith, or the parallel extended (21–28) ; and the personal appeal (29–37). The first two stanzas were /87/ written in pencil on the verso of a sheet of Arnold's notes for his 'Empedocles.' The third appears on the same sheet but at the side of the page: ". . . of the world. Ah love &c." This might suggest that the whole was put together out of three separate parts: the first twenty lines, the last nine lines, and the intervening eight lines added as a link. This would surprise no one in view of Arnold's early letter to his sister, "myself am fragments"; nor is it inconsistent with what one may suppose to be a common practice of poets. It suggested to Tinker and Lowry, however, that the concluding stanza was the first part written and the preceding twenty-eight lines added as a "prelude." In any case, there is an easy and natural movement from beginning to end of the finished poem, and with one reservation a sufficient consistency.

---

[2] E. K. Chambers, *Matthew Arnold, A Study.* Oxford, 1947, p. 59. There is a kind of factual corroboration in the meteorological data. Arnold was married on 10 June 1851. The moon was full about 7 p.m. on the thirteenth and rose at 6:49 p.m.; therefore on any evening of the week following his wedding he could have seen the moon lying "fair Upon the straits" at Dover. High water at London Bridge was at 0:35 a.m., 1:00 p.m.; at Dover it would be a little later. The *Gentleman's Magazine* for July 1851 reports the weather as "fair, rain" for 11–13 June and as "fine, do." for 14–17 June. To be sure, poets are not held accountable for meteorological exactitude; but the setting of 'Dover Beach' has a factual air, and if the poem was written in or of mid-June 1851 it seems clear that Arnold's details are correct.

Nevertheless this movement is not altogether simple, as is evident from certain misunderstandings which readers and commentators have revealed.

The seascape—calm, high tide, the cliffs looking "vast" in the moonlight—gives the key. But[3] there is the beating of the surf, "the grating roar Of pebbles," the "tremulous cadence"[4] which adds "The eternal note of sadness" to the scene. As /88/ illustration that the note is eternal Arnold instances Sophocles, his favorite tragic poet. This same wash of the sea against the shore had made the same impression on Sophocles: it had reminded him, even as it reminds us in the north, of "the turbid ebb and flow Of human misery." Here one must be cautious. Arnold does not say that Sophocles compared the vicissitudes of life to the ebb and flow of the Aegean tides; nor has anyone ever found in the seven extant plays or in the numerous fragments any such comparison; nor was Sophocles likely to have made such a comparison, because there is little tide in the Aegean. The alleged parallels simply do not meet the case; they are irrelevant. In *Antigone* 583 ff. he compares the curse of heaven on a family to the Thracian sea-winds stirring up the sand and beating against the headlands. In *The Trachinian Maidens* III ff. he compares the changes in Heracles' life to the billow after billow of the storm winds. In *Oedipus at Colonus* he has the Chorus say that Oedipus is like a cape lashed by winds and waves. These and other passages may have been vaguely in Arnold's memory. They are, anyway, not strikingly original or recondite. Certainly they would not justify Arnold in saying what he has been supposed to say but did not say. For what Arnold says is that Sophocles, who knew the Aegean Sea, not the English Channel, hearing the surf beat on the shore felt the same sadness over the

---

[3] "Only" (line 7) must bear this meaning; it goes with the semicolloquial tone of language and meter—up to the last stanza. The sea is calm, the night is still, except for . . . It results from Arnold's choice of his alternative epithets for "the night air." One of them, "hush'd," would have gone well with the first lines, but he chose the other, "sweet," probably as more appropriate with "Come to the window."

[4] *Tremulous*, for which the manuscript has *regular* with *mournful* as alternative, is an affective rather than a descriptive word. It occurs four times in Arnold's verse. It has descriptive value in 'The Strayed Reveller,' line 282:

> Ah, the cool night-wind, tremulous stars!
> Ah, glimmering water,
> Fitful earth-murmur. . . .

The echoes of this in 'Dover Beach' are interesting.

alternations of the human lot.[5] It is Arnold and not Sophocles who
/89/ uses the metaphor of the tides, a metaphor suggested by the
view and sound from his window at Dover.

Perhaps "metaphor of the tides" is itself a misleading phrase, for
there is only one tide in the text of the poem, the full or high tide.
But most readers (like Tinker and Lowry: "the ebb and flow of the
sea at Dover") have been led astray by "ebb and flow Of human
misery." Perhaps Arnold is partly responsible for the confusion, and
one or two words require special attention. There is no difficulty
with "it":

> Sophocles long ago
> Heard it on the Ægæan—

heard the "tremulous cadence slow," the rhythm of the waves breaking and drawing back. This ordinarily we see rather than hear, but
the time is night and on a pebbly beach there is a "grating roar" or
at least a distinct noise as the waves withdraw; and this Arnold likens
to the larger movement of the ebb and flow of tides. In line 8 the
manuscript had

> Where the sea meets the moon-blanched sand.

The last word was changed in 1880 to "land," obviously to avoid the
inconsistency of sand and pebbles ("shingles," line 28). But for "sea"
the first printing, 1867, had "ebb," which remained through three
editions and was not changed to "sea" until 1880. This is of course
an improvement, for at Dover, *in the poem*, the sea is always at high
tide. But the idea was present in Arnold's mind and appears nine lines
below in "ebb and flow Of human misery," which is still not tides
but the forward and retreating movement of waves on the beach.

---

[5] Since nothing has been adduced from Sophocles which at all resembles this
"thought," viz., the alternations of joy and misery compared to the motion of waves
on the shore, it is likely that Arnold chose the name—so much more definite
than "a Greek" in the Grande Chartreuse poem—because Sophocles *was* his
favorite tragic poet, "The mellow glory of the Attic stage." Any tragedy of course
moves from prosperity to disaster, but not back and forth like the waves. Euripides
might have been a better choice for accuracy, if a kind of melancholy pessimism
is implied in the comparison, but not for sound or associative value.—A sort of
parallel to Arnold's use of Sophocles has been suggested to me in Keats' use of
Ruth in 'Ode to a Nightingale.' Both Sophocles and Ruth carry the reader back
in time, and as there is nothing in the Greek texts about "the ebb and flow Of
human misery," so there is no nightingale in the *Book of Ruth*.

The sound of this movement produces in "us" at Dover /90/ "a thought"—presumably that of the next stanza, namely, that Faith, which was once like a full tide, has now ebbed. So that now, in imagination

> *I only hear*
> *Its melancholy, long, withdrawing roar,*
> *Retreating.*

The two images, the ebb and flow of waves and the ebb and flow of tides are blended, or rather, the one is imaginatively extended to become the other; and

> *the grating roar*
> *Of pebbles which the waves draw back*

is transformed to the retreating movement of the tide, as the Sea of Faith recedes. Arnold does not see and hear this literally; he expands the metaphor, just as he enlarges the surf at Dover to include

> *the vast edges drear*
> *And naked shingles of the* [whole] *world.*

There is another small difficulty:

> *The Sea of Faith*
> *Was once, too, at the full;*

that is, *as* the actual tide at Dover is now high, *so* the Sea of Faith was at one time in the past at high tide; but not now. This does not mean, as it might mean, that in the time of Sophocles the Sea of Faith was at high tide. The word "too" does not refer to the fifth century B.C., but to the Dover tide in, say, 1851. Perhaps it is not supersubtle to see in "too" also an anticipation of the concluding stanza: we, Arnold and his bride, were full of faith when we married, and may we remain so in spite of the "confused alarms" which we shall presently face. "Let us be true To one another!" through the darkness and joylessness of the world before us. The sequence of images, /91/ feelings, and ideas is thus simple and natural and with reasonable care not difficult to follow.

But Arnold was not content with this; his weakness for ending on a high note was too strong for him.[6] In the last three lines he brought

---

6 This would be true, in a slightly different sense, if the last stanza was written before the rest; for in putting the parts together Arnold allowed the disturbing metaphor to stand.

in a new image, apparently to intensify the dark picture of human misery but confusing and inappropriate because, as everyone feels, it shifts our interest and attention from the sea imagery, which has been dominant hitherto, to one of "a darkling plain, Where ignorant armies clash by night." This is the one structural blemish of the poem. The critics have also darkened counsel by their search for sources. For the sea of faith we are referred to a passage in Sainte-Beuve; and this is interesting at least because it was noted by three different readers independently.[7] Sainte-Beuve, who was of course one of Arnold's favorite authors, set down, near Aigues-Mortes, on the Gulf of Lyons, in 1839 this *pensée*:

> Mon âme est pareille à ces plages où l'on dit que saint Louis s'est embarqué: la mer et la foi se sont depuis longtemps, helas! retirées, et c'est tout si parfois, à travers les sables, sous l'aride chaleur ou le froid mistral, je trouve un instant à m'asseoir à l'ombre d'un rare tamarin.[8]

This may safely be regarded as a parallel 'thought'—the sea and faith have, alas, long since withdrawn—rather than one which gave Arnold the necessary hint for his poem or even two lines of it. /92/

A fragment of Empedocles is of interest only because the last stanza of 'Dover Beach' is found among Arnold's notes for his 'Empedocles on Etna.' It will hardly be taken as a source or even as a suggestion for the battle imagery of the stanza. The most that could be urged is that it might have reminded him of the passage in Thucydides. It has been translated as follows: "The joyless land where are Murder and Wrath and the tribes of other Dooms, and Wasting Diseases and Corruptions and the Works of Dissolution wander over the Meadow of Disaster in the darkness."[9]

In 413 B.C. the Athenians and their Greek allies brought a fleet to Sicily and in the attack on Syracuse engaged the enemy on the hill of Epipolae. "Now it seemed impossible," Thucydides narrates;

> Now it seemed impossible to approach the heights in the daytime . . . and after the first watch, . . . they got by the Syracusan guards without

---

[7] Clarence C. Clark, "A Possible Source of Matthew Arnold's *Dover Beach*," *MLN*, XVII (1902), 484–85; Arnold Whitridge, "Matthew Arnold and Sainte-Beuve," *PMLA*, LIII (1935), 303–13; 307–308, with no reference to Clark; I. E. Sells, *Matthew Arnold and France. The Poet*, Cambridge, 1935, who got it from Babbitt, *Masters of Modern French Criticism*, New York, 1912, p. 104.

[8] *Portraits littéraires*, new ed., Paris 1864, III, 540.

[9] Kathleen Freeman, *Ancilla to The Pre-Socratic Philosophers*, Oxford, 1946; Empedocles, Fragment 121.

being observed, . . . and killed some of the guards; most of these, however, fled at once to the camps, of which there were three upon Epipolae
. . . and brought word of the attack, informing also the six hundred
Syracusans who were posted as an advanced guard. . . . These hastened
at once to the rescue, but Demosthenes and the Athenians met them and
put them to rout despite their vigorous resistance. This body of Athenians then straightway pressed forward . . . ; while another party at the
very first proceeded to seize the cross-wall of the Syracusans, ... But
the Syracusans and their allies . . . came up from the outworks; yet,
since this daring attempt had been made upon them unexpectedly at
night, they were still dazed as they attacked the Athenians and were at
first forced back by them. But while the Athenians were by now going
forward, in some disorder, considering themselves victorious and wish-
ing as quickly as possible to push their way through all the enemy's
forces that had not yet been engaged, . . . it was the Boeotians who first
made a stand against them, and by making a charge routed and put
them to flight. /93/

XLIV. By this time the Athenians were getting into a state of so great
confusion and perplexity that it has not been easy to learn from either
side just how the several events occurred . . . . in a battle by night—
the only one that took place in this war between large armies—how
could anyone know anything clearly? For though there was a bright
moon, they could only see one another, as it is natural to do in moonlight—seeing before them the vision of a person but mistrusting their
recognition of their own friends. There were, besides, large numbers of
hoplites belonging to both sides moving about in a narrow space. And
on the Athenian side, some were already defeated, while others, still
in their first onset, were advancing unchecked; but of the rest of the
army a large portion had only just finished the ascent and others were
still coming up, so that they did not know which body to join. For the
front lines were already all in confusion in consequence of the rout
that had taken place, and the two sides were difficult to distinguish by
reason of the outcries. The Syracusans and their allies, as they were win-
ning, were cheering one another and indulging in no little shouting—it
being impossible in the night to communicate in any other way—while at
the same time they held their ground against their assailants; the Athenians were trying to find their own comrades, and regarded as hostile
what came from the opposite direction, even though it might be a party of
friends belonging to the troops already in flight, and as they were constantly calling out the demand for the watchword, the only means they
had of distinguishing friend from foe, they not only caused much confusion in their own ranks, everybody making the demand at the same
time, but also made their watchword known to the enemy. . . . [etc.,
etc.] . . . And so finally, when once they had been thrown into confusion,

coming into collision with their own comrades in many different parts of the army, friends with friends and citizens with fellow-citizens, they not only became panicstricken but came to blows with one another and were with difficulty separated. And as they were being pursued by the enemy many hurled themselves down from the bluffs and perished. . . .[10]

There is every reason to suppose, though no positive evi- /94/ dence, that Arnold had read Thucydides at Rugby. (His father had edited the *History*, 1830–35.) And this passage is the most likely source, if a source must be found, for the closing image of 'Dover Beach.' He need not have returned to the text; a general recollection of the story would have been enough. Clough used a similar reference in 'The Bothie,' but Arnold, unlike Clough, did not include the "watchword," and he substituted "darkling plain" (as though to suit with the setting at Dover) for the hill of Epipolae; but the rest, the tone and the confusion of armies, is all there in Thucydides.[11]

II

The meter of 'Dover Beach,' for all its apparent simplicity and ease, is more subtle than one might think. The four stanzas differ in length, but the second and third together (which form a unit of meaning, a contrast to the first stanza), are of the same length as the first. Line 9 of the first stanza has to wait till the third stanza for its answering rime (*roar : shore : roar*). The fourth stanza repeats the rime word *light* (lines 3, 33) and so the *a*-rimes of the first stanza. In this way the first two and the last stanzas are interlinked by rime. There is some parallelism in the arrangement of rimes. The opening pattern *aba* recurs as *dbd* and *gfg* in the first stanza, and carries over to the second stanza: *aba cbc*. The third stanza differs from all the others. The fourth is the most regular and goes something like the octave of a sonnet: *abba cddc*, plus the last rime, /95/ *c*, repeated with a kind of coda effect. It need not be supposed that these are all carefully contrived devices, but they contribute to, as they offset, the seemingly natural flow of the whole poem. The variations in length

---

[10] Thucydides, VII, xliii-xliv. Trans. Charles F. Smith, Loeb ed., London 1923, IV, 83–91.

[11] It has been supposed that Arnold took the incident from Clough rather than direct from the Greek. See Paul Turner, "*Dover Beach* and the *Bothie of Tober-na-Vuolich*," *English Studies*, XXVIII (1947), 173–78. The idea is that Arnold disagreed with the wishful thinking of the '*Bothie*' and composed a fragment of nine lines to express his disagreement; but withheld the (finished) poem till 1867 lest Clough (d. 1861) should be offended. See also Buckner B. Trawick, "The Sea of Faith and the Battle by Night in *Dover Beach*," *PMLA*, LXV (1950), 1282–83.

of line are similarly subtle. Measured by stresses, the first runs 345 555 444 5454 4; the second 355 345; the third 255 353 54; the fourth consists of seven 5-stress lines introduced by a 3-stress and concluded by a 4-stress line. All four stanzas begin with a short line: 3, 3, 2, 3. Three of the four stanzas end with a 4-stress line. The 555 444 54 54 grouping of the first stanza is echoed by the 54 endings of the third and fourth stanzas. Moreover, twenty of the thirty-seven lines as printed are 5-stress lines; but besides these there are several examples of concealed blank verse:

> *The sea is calm to-night. The tide is full*
> *on the French coast the light Gleams and is gone*
> *the cliffs of England stand, Glimmering and vast*
> *and fling, At their return, up the high strand*
> *and bring The eternal note of sadness in.*
> *The Sea of Faith Was once, too, at the full*
> *Retreating to the breath Of the night-wind*
> *Ah, love, let us be true To one another!*

Others might pass as blank verse:

> *Listen! you hear the grating roar Of pebbles*
> *the turbid ebb and flow Of human misery.*

Or this last could be read as an alexandrine, and so also

> *With tremulous cadence slow and bring The eternal note*
> *Sophocles long ago Heard it on the Ægæan*
> *which seems To lie before us like a land of dreams.*

These combinations or variations confirm the smoothness of the rhythm alongside the apparent irregularity of the line-length;[12] and at the same time the interweaving of shorter and /96/ longer lines produces something of the effect of waves breaking and retreating, of "ebb and flow."

---

[12] The meter of 'Philomela' is less varied. Of its thirty-two lines, five are 2-stress, eleven are 3-stress, and eleven are 5-stress. Lines 1–2 and 14–15 together make blank verse and there are two concealed in
> *And can this fragrant lawn With its cool trees*
> *and feel come over thee, Poor fugitive.*
The poem is ostensibly unrimed, but two lines (4 and 8) end with *pain* and two (7 and 14) with *brain*; and lines 23, 26 have a conventional rime (*thee : agony*).

U. C. Knoepflmacher

Dover Revisited:
The Wordsworthian Matrix in
the Poetry of Matthew Arnold*

Much has been written on Matthew Arnold's qualification of Romanticism, on his fluctuating estimates of the English Romantic poets in general and of William Wordsworth in particular. Such studies are generally limited to Arnold's critical opinions.[1] Only occasionally, and then very succinctly, have students of Arnold's poetry dwelled on his creation of what a recent and perceptive critic has called "ironic echoes of Wordsworth": "a version of Wordsworth which is also a criticism and a rejection of Wordsworth's view."[2]

Arnold's poetry is, to a large extent, derivative. It draws on the classics for much of its mythic substance and the stateliness of its rhythm; on Goethe for intellectual content; on sources as remote as the *Bhagavad Gita* for that "wider application" which Arnold felt was "the one thing wanting to make Wordsworth an even greater poet than he is." But the core of Arnold's emotional power is Wordsworthian, and it is so by intent and not by mere coincidence. Arnold's poems avail themselves of situations that are Wordsworthian, images that are Wordsworthian, phrases that are Wordsworthian. This Wordsworthian matrix is enlisted in what essentially amounts to a denial of the vision of Arnold's predecessor, although, at the very same

---

* Reprinted from *Victorian Poetry*, I (1963), 17–26, by permission of the journal and the author.

[1] Among the more recent studies see D. G. James, *Matthew Arnold and the Decline of English Romanticism* (Oxford, 1961), and William A. Jamison, *Arnold and the Romantics* (Copenhagen, 1958).

[2] W. Stacy Johnson, *The Voices of Matthew Arnold: An Essay in Criticism* (New Haven, 1961), pp. 48, 47. See also Paull F. Baum, *Ten Studies in the Poetry of Matthew Arnold* (Durham, 1958), p. 25f: Lionel Trilling, *Matthew Arnold* (New York, 1955), pp. 75ff: and E. D. H. Johnson, *The Alien Vision of Victorian Poetry* (Princeton, 1952), pp. 152–153.

time, it is relied upon to preserve Wordsworth's ability "to make us feel." I shall try to illustrate the quality and extent of Arnold's use of this matrix in the two sections that follow by examining two poems, "Resignation" and "Dover Beach," in the light of their counterparts in Wordsworth. I shall conclude by discussing the reasons which prompted Arnold to conserve Wordsworthian elements in his poetry /18/ in face of the almost impassable gulf which separated his convictions as a Victorian poet from those of his Romantic precursor.

I

Arnold's "Resignation" is his version, or, more properly, his inversion, of Wordsworth's "Tintern Abbey." The parallelism between the two poems is deliberate. It enables Arnold to employ his predecessor's work as a frame of reference, an ironic "touchstone" essential to his own meaning.[3] "Resignation" is almost twice as long as "Tintern Abbey." It abounds in erudite allusions and echoes from sources as varied as Lucretius and Goethe. But the core of the poem is unmistakably Wordsworthian: the setting is the Lake County of the Romantics; the situation, a return to the earlier associations of the scene by a matured poet and his sister; the import, a creed handed down by the poet to his listener.

In "Tintern Abbey" Wordsworth and Dorothy stand "here upon the banks of this fair river." The poet mourns his lost childhood oneness with Nature but derives joy from the knowledge that his sister still possesses the power that he has lost. The poem ends on a triumphant assertion of his belief in a matured and "sober pleasure" based on the "wild ecstasies" of youth. Memory becomes a source of joy: "Nature never did betray the heart that loved her." The poet, "a worshiper of Nature," can readily become its priest.

In "Resignation" the poet and his sister also stand "on this mild bank above the stream," amidst a lush natural landscape which has remained unaltered despite the changes they have suffered. "The loose

---

[3] In their otherwise excellent commentary on the poetry of Arnold, C. B. Tinker and H. F. Lowry, though dwelling extensively on the Goethean sources of "Resignation," strangely enough fail to point out that the poem is above all a rebuttal of Wordsworth, who, according to his youthful critic, "should have read more books, among them, no doubt those of the Goethe whom he disparaged without reading him." Only Professor Baum seems to have taken notice of the analogies between "Resignation" and "Tintern Abbey." But he dismisses them cursorily by remarking that the " 'exhortations' " of the poets are after all "quite unlike" each other, thus underestimating the importance of this "unlikeness" for a reading of Arnold's poem (*Ten Studies*, pp. 25–26, fn. 3).

dark stones" have not moved; "this wild brook" runs on, undisturbed. The scene's permanence sharpens the poet's awareness of his own mutability. He, too, hopes to derive a creed based on his observation of Nature. But while Arnold's yearning for sobering "thoughts" suggested by the surroundings is not unlike Wordsworth's, his interpretation of these surroundings is markedly different. Indeed, the ethical creed that he charts out for his sister and the poetic creed he indirectly prescribes for himself are based on a complete re-definition of a Wordworthian faith in Nature. To Wordsworth, the communion between Nature and man is in itself an abundant compensation for the mutability of life—it brings about a communion between /19/ brother and sister, man and man, and confirms the poet in his role of Nature's high priest. To Arnold, on the other hand, the utter impersonality of the scene before him only accentuates the need for an adequate attitude towards a natural world which can no more provide the "tender joy" that Wordsworth was capable of extracting from it than it can act as a stimulus for the heightened sensations sought by his Faustian sister. He must therefore explain to the Romantic Fausta the limitations suggested by the landscape, and, simultaneously, delimit his own functions as new kind of poet, a poet deprived of the "rapt security" inherent in the Romantic vision.

To Arnold the landscape is but an emblem of "the general life," an impersonal power which demands the submission of all men. But rather than becoming a mere object subjected to the capriciousness of "chance," man can achieve the dignity of a rule by "fate" if he understands his own position within the "dizzying eddy" of life. This understanding can come only through detachment. It is achieved instinctively by gypsies plodding in their "hereditary way"; it is achieved consciously by those higher beings who can discern through a special insight "what through experience others learn." In outline, Arnold's schematization is not unlike Wordsworth's. He has identified the landscape before him with an order or plan which he, as a detached observer, is able to perceive; he has maintained that this order can be understood instinctively by some and consciously by others; he has established the need for an acceptance of this plan, "the general life." But, of course, it is the valuation which Arnold places on these elements which is entirely opposed to Wordsworth's. Children unconsciously in touch with the divine have become gypsies instinctively attuned to the buffets of life; the redeeming Dorothy has become the unredeemable Fausta; the isolated poet who converts the "still, sad music of humanity" into a joyful faith has become a detached stoic contemplator, content with a "sad lucidity of soul."[4] For what has changed, above all, is the order perceived by the poet and the manner in which the poet's perception has been achieved.

The divine "presence" perceived by Wordsworth resides in the landscape he sees, as well as in himself. It is: /20/

> a sense sublime
> Of something far more deeply interfused,
> Whose dwelling is the light of setting suns,
> And the round ocean and the living air,
> And the blue sky, and in the mind of man;
> A motion and a spirit, that impels
> All living things, all objects of all thought,
> And rolls through all things.

To Arnold, on the other hand, "the something which infects the world" is not an invisible *primum mobile*. It is the aggregate of all that is visible, an impersonal and tyrannical power which offers "not joy, but peace" to him who apprehends its operations:

> Before him he sees life unroll,
> A placid and continuous whole—
> That general life, which does not cease,
> Whose secret is not joy, but peace;
> That life, whose dumb wish is not miss'd
> If birth proceeds, if things subsist;
> The life of plants, and stones, and rain,
> The life he craves—if not in vain
> Fate gave, what chance shall not control,
> His sad lucidity of soul.

---

[4] Arnold's choice of the gypsies as his prime example is extremely significant. His justification of the gypsies to the sister who dismisses them as being "less" than "man" is nothing less than a direct rebuttal of the position taken by Wordsworth in his 1807 poem, "Gipsies." In this little-known poem, Wordsworth regards the gypsies he has met during an excursion as sub-human, almost devilish creatures who are unaffected by the laws of man and Nature. Shunning their fellowmen during the day, totally oblivious of their natural surroundings, Wordsworth's gypsies raise "bolder" fires at night and thus defy the "mighty Moon" and the "very stars" that "reprove" them for their negligence as much as the poet himself. Arnold's gypsies likewise "crouch round the wild flame." But their purpose is simple: they merely want to stay warm in order to "rub through" life. For, unlike Wordsworth's gypsies, they *are* affected by time and change. Their indifference to Nature therefore is not, as with Wordsworth, a reprehensible act of defiance, but, quite to the contrary, represents an expression of their triumph over a natural world which has, in turn, become wholly indifferent towards them. Arnold's gypsies wait stoically "Till death arrive to supersede, / For them, vicissitude and need."

Nature has provided Wordsworth with a "holy love"; it has only confirmed Arnold's saddened intellectual awareness.

"Resignation" and "Tintern Abbey" rely on the modulation of conflicting moods; both poems conclude on the speaker's subjection to a discipline based on Nature. Wordsworth emphasizes the beneficence of this discipline; Arnold emphasizes its grim necessity. In each case, the landscape has acted as a guide. But while for Wordsworth Nature is an active teacher and comforter who readily reveals "a presence that disturbs me with the joy of elevated thoughts," Arnold's "thoughts" are addressed rhetorically to the impassive landscape before him so that it might confirm his own well-rehearsed lesson in the art of "bearing":

> Enough, we live!—and if a life,
> With large results so little rife,
> Though bearable, seem hardly worth
> This pomp of worlds, the pain of birth;
> Yet, Fausta, the mute turf we tread,
> The solemn hills around us spread,
> The stream which falls incessantly,
> The strange-scrawl'd rocks, the lonely sky,
> If I might lend their life a voice,
> Seem to bear rather than rejoice.

The lesson of joy given to Wordsworth is thus subverted. For Arnold's Nature is utterly impervious to the emotional demands of its students. "The meadows and the woods and mountains" speak freely to Wordsworth in the "language of sense." Arnold, however, must scrupulous-/21/ ly point out that the language he ascribes to the scene before him is really his own. The turf is "mute," the hills are "solemn," even the rocks are enigmatic and "strange-scrawl'd." The poet thus is forced to superimpose his own order on the scene he sees before him. He can at best attribute an imagined "voice" to the life he sees around him; he can only assume that the landscape would "*seem*" to teach him how to bear.

Wordsworth's vision is transcendent and symbolical: ocean, air, and sky contain the same spirit which dwells "in the mind of man." Arnold's vision is analytical and allegorical: the mind of man can tentatively impose its understanding upon what it apprehends through the senses. Therefore, while Wordsworth's poet is a medium for the divine plan of Nature, Arnold's poet is merely the interpreter of the "dumb" wishes of a neutral universe. Whereas Wordsworth becomes infused and intoxicated by the centrifugal power of Nature, Arnold must stand aside and examine his own relative position in time and space in order to preserve his "lucidity of soul." The scene before him is meaningless in itself. It must be related to Mohammedan pilgrims and Gothic warriors, to Orpheus and to Homer. Intensity is replaced by extensiveness: *"Not deep the poet sees, but wide."* The resolution of Arnold's poem therefore depends entirely on his a *priori* survey of the "general life," a survey brought about by precisely that cultural view which Wordsworth lacked to make "his thought richer and his influence of wider application."

"Resignation" thus represents Arnold's attempt to give a contemporary "application" to Wordworth's Romantic poem. It is a characteristically Victorian juggling of "heart" and "head": an emotional faith in Nature is qualified by the wider intellectual view afforded by scientific skepticism, historicism, and "Culture." Arnold's qualification also alters Wordsworth's poetic method. The symbolically exalted "green pastoral landscape" becomes an allegorized "green hill-side" arbitrarily invested with qualities corresponding to the human situation. This same process is carried over, eighteen years later, into "Dover Beach" (1867), a poem in which Arnold again relies on a "Wordsworthian matrix" to record his own dissentient Victorian vision.

II

While Arnold's "Resignation" stands squarely in the line of "Tintern Abbey," the dependence of "Dover Beach" on Wordsworth's two famous sonnets, "It Is a Beauteous Evening, Calm and Free," and "Near Dover, September, 1802," is of a more oblique nature. Still, the analogies are striking. For Arnold draws on the situation, the imagery, and the phrasing of both of Wordsworth's Romantic sonnets /22/ to build up the essentially anti-Romantic impact of "Dover Beach."

In "A Beauteous Evening" Wordsworth interprets the scene for "the dear girl" at his side by asking her to listen to the thunder of the tide:

> Listen! the mighty Being is awake,
> And doth with his eternal motion make
> A sound like thunder—everlastingly.

Arnold's command to his companion echoes that of the sonnet, but, significantly enough, his interpretation of the sound is almost exactly the opposite of Wordsworth's:

> Listen! you hear the grating roar
> Of pebbles which the waves draw back, and fling,
> At their return, up the high strand,
> Begin, and cease, and then again begin,
> With tremulous cadence slow, and bring
> The eternal note of sadness in.

To Wordsworth the sound of the sea suggests a "solemn thought" which, though important for his own edification, is unnecessary for the child who is in direct communion with the divine order of Nature. Arnold likewise finds "in the sound a thought," but he must translate his thought to his companion, who has, like the poet himself, been deceived by the illusory beauty of the calm evening scene. Thus, while the "thunder" of the sea suggests to Wordsworth the beneficence of Nature's plan and fills him with that harmonious sound described in "Tintern Abbey" as "The still, sad music of humanity, / Not harsh nor grating," it is precisely the "grating" quality of the tide's "roar" which causes Arnold to reflect on the "ebb and flow of human misery" heard long ago by Sophocles.

Arnold makes use of Wordsworth's second sonnet, "Near Dover," to an even larger extent. At first sight, however, only the similarity in location would seem to link both poems. While "A Beauteous Evening" and "Dover Beach" share a common situation provided by the seaside setting, the evening, the relationship between the speaker and his companion, and by the interpretation of what the poet *hears* rather than sees, in "Near Dover" the poet is alone out in the open; it is daylight; and the poet's interpretation is based exclusively on the unusually sharp visual clarity which projects the French coast into an unexpected proximity:

> Inland, within a hollow vale, I stood,
> And saw, while sea was calm and air was clear,
> The coast of France—the coast of France how near!

Only the calmness of the sea is identical in both poems:

> The sea is calm to-night.
> The tide is full, the moon lies fair
> Upon the straits;—on the French coast the light
> Gleams and is gone.

/23/ The sharply delineated "coast of France" of "Near Dover" has become a shimmering "French coast." Moonlight haze has been substituted for daylight clarity. And, what is more, the heightened, quasi-

Wordsworthian feelings produced by the sight of the "tranquil bay" are abruptly replaced by the thoughts produced by the "grating" roar. For "Dover Beach" inverts the experience depicted in "Near Dover" just as much as "Resignation" inverts "Tintern Abbey."

Wordsworth's poem is a poem about belief. The contracting channel brings the coast of France into a "frightful neighborhood" but the span of waters which divides the two countries acts as a protective ring which speaks to the poet of the unseen protection of God:

> I shrunk; for verily the barrier flood
> Was like a lake, or river bright and fair,
> A span of waters; yet what power is there!
> What mightiness for evil and for good!
> Even so doth God protect us if we be
> Virtuous and wise.

The sonnet posits a faith in the invisible which is based on a faith in the visible. "Dover Beach" laments the impossibility of such a faith. Just as in "Resignation" Arnold discredits the "healing power" of a Wordsworthian landscape, so, in "Dover Beach," he stresses the unreliability of a Romantic belief in the visual.

Wordsworth's sonnet is neatly divided. The octave renders the poet's surprise at the sudden proximity of the French coast; the sestet, beginning with "even so," reproduces the intuitive faith which the awareness of the "barrier flood" has produced. The opening of "Dover Beach" mimics Wordsworth's harmonious vision. Like Wordsworth's octave, the first eight lines of "Dover Beach" rely exclusively on the poet's visual appreciation of the scene before him. The smooth alliteration and balance of Wordsworth's "and saw *while* sea *was* calm and air *was* clear" find their counterpart in Arnold's "The tide is *full*, the moon *lies* fair." Just as the sight of the water provokes from Wordsworth an enthusiastic outcry over its "power," so does the view of the bay cause Arnold to indulge in a romantic exclamation. But the evidence of the senses is soon dispelled. The poet's raptures are qualified by a hesitant "only" in line seven and by a sudden pause after line eight, as the full force of the "thought" provoked by the "grating roar" has asserted itself. From that point on, discordance enters into the poem. The rhyme scheme and rhythm become highly irregular and regain only some regularity in the conclusion.

For Wordsworth, the optical trick which transforms the channel into a "river bright and fair" provides an instantaneous revelation, a realization of God's decree. But for Arnold, the momentary deception produced by the "fair" moon and the glimmering coastal lights /24/ only confirms his anterior suspicion of the senses. For neither a visual sense, as in "Near Dover," nor an auditory sense, as in "A Beauteous Evening," can be relied upon, since these senses may very well be at odds. Thus, sight is replaced by sound, but sound must be replaced by thought, by the poet's self-conscious allegorization of the retreating waters into a "Sea of Faith." The emotional Wordsworthian surge of the opening lines has demanded a counter-movement; the flow of feeling has been displaced by the ebb of intellect. Wordsworth's analogy between the bright "barrier flood" and God's armor has been instinctive; Arnold's analogy between the sea and the "bright girdle" which was once furled around the shores of humanity is derivative and intellectualized. The "thought" that he has found in the harsh sound of the tide is not the product of a sudden inspiration, but is based instead on his lulled, but now re-awakened, consciousness of historical determinism, the decay of religion, of Sophocles' metaphoric description of human misery, and, indirectly, of that other poet who stood before him "by this distant northern sea." Once again Arnold has inserted the "Culture" he found absent in Wordsworth.

For Wordsworth, the contraction of the channel causes him to "shrink" with it into a more direct contact with God. For Arnold, the channel spreads out endlessly through time and space leaving him stranded on "the naked shingles of the world." Wordsworth regards the winds and waters of the channel as messengers of God's "decree." "In themselves," he asserts, they "are nothing." Arnold must cling to this "nothing." The value he ascribes to the "bright girdle" of water is the same value given to it by Wordsworth. But the emblem has only an antiquarian importance. It has lost its immediacy and become a thing of the past. Resigning himself to life in a "land of dreams," the poet can at least bemoan his inability to believe in the dream itself, the dream of the Romantics. For in his catalogue of lost qualities—joy, love, light, certitude, peace, and help for pain—Arnold enumerated all the qualities that Wordsworth was still able to obtain in 1802, near the very same beach. The view from Dover had changed considerably over the short span of sixty years.

III

"Resignation" and "Dover Beach" are perhaps the most obvious examples of Arnold's use of a Wordsworthian matrix in his poetry. But they are by no means the only ones. Arnold's "To a Gipsy Child by the Seashore" reverberates with echoes from the "Immortality" ode;[5] his "East London" and "West London" sonnets are the Victo-

---

[5] Cf. W. Stacy Johnson, pp. 47–51.

rian counterparts of the London sonnets written by Wordsworth in 1802; /25/ the conception of the "Marguerite" poems owes much to Wordsworth's use of his "Lucy." There are correspondences in situations and phrases. Images, such as the elm-tree in "Thyrsis" (which recalls the oak of "Michael") or the "sea of life" in "To Marguerite," are invested with Wordsworthian properties.

The introduction of these elements into Arnold's own poetry represents more than a mere negation of Wordsworth's vision. There is a definite effort at conservation on the part of a poet, who, according to Quiller-Couch's witticism, had a notable tendency to regard himself as "Wordsworth's widow."[6] The younger man, whose boyhood "had been spent in the Lake Country and under Wordsworth's affectionate eye,"[7] tried to knit on his own experience to that of his predecessor. For not only Arnold, but a host of other eminent Victorians, regarded Wordsworth with a curious ambivalence. Intellectually, they deplored the simplicity of his natural faith; yet, at the same time, the skeleton of his faith provided them with a vicarious emotional gratification. For Wordsworth was able to do what his successcessors could no longer achieve. He could convert grief and pain into joyous affirmation; he could draw this affirmation from the element which he called "the still, sad music of humanity," and which Arnold was to re-name "the eternal note of sadness." This is the pattern of some of his greatest poems, "Tintern Abbey," the "Immortality" ode, the opening of *The Prelude*. Even in his "Elegiac Stanzas," written "in bereavement over the tragic death of the poet's dearly beloved brother," was he able to draw hope from suffering and to find soothing emotions by which he could "humanize" his soul. To the Victorians such a feat was definitely worth observing.

Arnold particularly admired this Wordsworthian power of transforming individual grief into a statement of universal affirmation. In his "Memorial Verses, April 1850," he pays homage to his dead predecessor by ranking him above Goethe and Byron. The attitude Arnold takes toward the Laureate is very similar to that which, ninety years later, W. H. Auden was to take towards Yeats. The deceased poet stands for a definite period of history, a simpler world-view which his successor cannot revive. But Wordsworth also stands for something else:

> Ah! since dark days still bring to light
> Man's prudence and man's fiery might,

---

[6] Quoted by Professor Douglas Bush in "Wordsworth and the Classics," *UTQ*, II (April, 1933), 359.

[7] Lionel Trilling, p. 19.

> Time may restore us in his course
> Goethe's sage mind and Byron's force;
> But where will Europe's latter hour
> Again find Wordsworth's healing power? /26/
> Others will teach us how to dare,
> And against fear our breast to steel;
> Others will strengthen us to bear—
> But who, ah! who, will make us feel?

Others can strengthen us to bear by preaching a "prudent" Goethean renunciation; others can teach us to resist despair through sheer vitality. But Wordsworth's "healing power" is as unretrievable as the shining armor of the Sea of Faith. The question of the hour, therefore, is not only "*who* will make us feel?" but also the implicit "*what* will make us feel?" Arnold never doubts that the power to "make us feel" must be kept alive at all costs; but from where is this feeling to be drawn? Nature no longer offers a religion. The Victorian poet can no longer expect to harmonize the "still, sad music of humanity" into a universal chorus of faith. He must therefore do the second best thing. He must cling to the "eternal note of sadness" itself. He can share it with Wordsworth and lament his own inability to replace this sadness with new feelings of joy, "Wordsworth's healing power." Thus, paradoxically enough, the Victorian poet can engender feeling by bemoaning the loss of feeling. He can preserve Wordsworth's emotional core.

Arnold eventually realized that such a diminished conservation of Wordsworth was not a conservation after all. For, by reiterating an elegiac "note of sadness," Arnold had transgressed against his own rules for "the right Art" by omitting the quality of joy, the joy so deeply felt by Wordsworth but denied to Arnold in "Resignation" and "Dover Beach." Arnold renounced poetry and turned to the dissemination of Culture. But even in his new role, he remained faithful to his desire to blend Wordsworth's feeling with the intellectualism of his own age. In 1879, nine years before his death, Arnold offered a selection of Wordsworth's poetry to the Victorian reading public. His revision of entire lines and phrases was regarded by some as a sign of editorial irresponsibility. It suggests, however, the extent to which Arnold had taken upon himself the cultural responsibility of preserving Wordsworth as an emotional fount for his age, a task he had already set for himself, long before, in the creation of his own poems.

R. M. Gollin

"Dover Beach": The Background of its Imagery*

'Dover Beach' is probably Matthew Arnold's finest short poem; certainly it has attracted more commentary than any other. Yet critics still seek to ascertain its unifying theme, and scholars have yet to find its precise relevance to its own time. This study approaches these problems in a manner not previously attempted, examination of the particular spiritual predicament defined by the figurative tradition from which Arnold drew the poem's primary images.

The problem of thematic unity can be defined briefly. 'Dover Beach' /494/ is essentially a dramatic soliloquy in which a man standing before a window surveys a calm, moonlit shore, hears in the sound of surf-tossed pebbles an echo of human suffering endlessly repeated, and arrives at a similar metaphorical 'thought', a vision of humanity left helplessly exposed by the tidal recession of the great 'Sea of Faith'. Then, after a sudden outcry to his listener the speaker presents a final terrifying image of all mankind trapped together in the chaos of a benighted battlefield. His progress of thought implies an organic relationship between the sea image and the battle image, the latter serving as a summary climax to the 'thought' figured forth by its predecessor.

Indeed, the poem exhibits several kinds of unity: it moves slowly from a dream of innocent natural appearances to a fearful figurative vision of the world inhabited when one wakens to reality; it gradually changes in mood from tranquillity through meditative sadness to desperation; and these movements are dominated by the continuously halting and surging rhythms of the irregular lines and rhymes with

* Reprinted from *English Studies*, XLVIII (December, 1967), 493–511, by permission of the journal and the author.

which the whole poem is composed. The two primary images are themselves superficially unified by associated details: enveloping darkness, the sound of roaring, grating and clashing, and perhaps even by a single implied movement of the eye from the shoreline to an imaginary battle on the plains above Dover. Yet the sea and battle images still lack significant congruence. The figurative men stranded on the edge of a tidal sea suffer communally, passively, and helplessly from regular, impersonal motion in the nature of things, the action of the waves and the night wind, bound by necessity. The men trapped in the confusion of the night battle suffer on the other hand from a self-created anarchy, from the random injuries they freely inflict on each other, a different predicament altogether. Again, the 'moon-blanch'd' night scene of the first image is not a condition for ignorant action, as is the dark night of the second. Even the crucial word 'Faith' remains only vaguely defined by the poem: it seems to mean little more than a state of total immersion uniting all men and protecting them from the discomfort of naked exposure. The poem does not tell us *what* faith, or faith *in what:* yet its recession results in two quite specifically delineated forms of suffering. Like the skew edges of a Cézanne table, the two unaligned figures force readers into continually renewed search for the poem's essential unity. Various unifying subjects seem to emerge: the problem of human isolation, the poignance of love in a treacherous world, the endless cycle of eternal returning which is history, and the themes of much great literature— free will and necessity, and illusion and reality. But none of these govern details in the whole poem, and only the most subtle and dedicated criticism can avoid concluding that however powerfully moving and suggestive, the work is imperfectly composed. Despite similar debate over the simile ending 'The Scholar Gipsy' one nevertheless hesitates to say that Arnold's final image here in a brief lyric as there in a long poem only approximately figures forth the poem's meaning.

Nor have we ascertained a particular historical setting for the poem. /495/ Its manuscript places it between 1849 and 1851,[1] between *The Strayed Reveller* and *Empedocles on Etna,* and it shares with these poems the young Arnold's concern with hopeful or tragic ac-

---

[1] All but the last stanza were written on the back of some early notes for 'Empedocles'; the last stanza apparently then already existed, since the extant manuscript concludes 'Ah love &c.' Datings based on Arnold's relationships with Marguerite or Miss Wightman are merely speculative; any based on a later possible source in St. Beuve—A. Whitridge, 'Matthew Arnold and St. Beuve', *PMLA,* LIII (1938), 303–313—have been superseded by discovery of earlier similar passages in other writers.

ceptance of a world in which the old sustaining verities have disappeared. But why Arnold felt they had disappeared is still far from
clear. Given his father's profoundly inclusive faith, speculation about
the aridity of eighteenth century orthodoxy, the superficiality of Victorian liberalism, or the irrelevance of Tractarian dogmatism is not
especially helpful; and it can be shown that however troubling other
men found the Higher Criticism, pre-Darwinian naturalism, and the
morality of such Christian doctrine, Dr. Arnold's theology had already
anticipated and circumvented these grounds for spiritual unrest.[2]
None of these need to have troubled his son. But unfortunately,
though we know much about the later Arnold's compensating beliefs,
there is only a scant biographical record for the years when he first
fell from his father's faith; we can only guess how he arrived at
'Dover Beach'.

Yet it is of special significance that the two primary images of
'Dover Beach' were commonplace in religious and political discussions during the 1830's and 1840's. Sea and battle imagery is, of course,
common to most literary and polemical traditions. But when these
images were used by Arnold's immediate circle, certain details were
stressed that are rarely found in other writing. These prior citations
usually point toward the predicament of men who cannot distinguish
wave from tidal movements but must, and men committed to chaotic
battle who dare not withdraw from the field. Moreover, examination
of these prior citations reveals that Arnold's immediate acquaintances
tended to use both images when discussing a single problem still
neglected by students of the Victorian period—the decline of faith
in the infallibility of conscience as a guide to religious and social
reform. Arnold knew that the images of 'Dover Beach' had been
sanctioned and given special meaning by their earlier uses, yet many
instances have never been called to our notice, and others have been
identified without comment on that meaning in context.[3] Like most

[2] Dr. Arnold's stabilizing influence on later religious modernism still awaits
study, but C. R. Sanders, *Coleridge and the Broad Church Movement* (Durham,
N.C., 1942) provides a summary of his views. H. Murphy, 'The Ethical Revolt
against Christian Orthodoxy', *AHR*, LX (July, 1955), 800–817, describes Victorian
revulsion against e.g. the morality of vicarious atonement, though without considering why many Victorians considered their own moral sense fit to judge Christian
morality. This paper suggests a reason.

[3] Some are given in C. B. Tinker and H. F. Lowry, *The Poetry of Matthew
Arnold: a Commentary* (London, 1940), pp. 173–178; B. Trawick, 'The Sea of
Faith and the Battle by Night in "Dover Beach"', PMLA, LXV (1950), 1282 f.;
and W. S. Johnson, 'Parallel Imagery in Arnold and Clough', *English Studies*,
XXXVII (1956), 1–11; the others discussed in this paper have not previously
been noticed as sources, antecedents, or analogues for those in 'Dover Beach'.

/496/ figurative traditions since the Romantic movement, the one in which 'Dover Beach' participates was for the most part personal and relatively short-lived. Yet like those of earlier ages, it can be ignored only at cost to our understanding of the poem's subject.

I.   Battle by Night

The night battle ending 'Dover Beach' fuses much human experience into a single scene: joyless, loveless, and pitiless struggle, isolation and danger in a world of chaotic disarray, and urgent duty turned self-defeating. As such, it is difficult not to read it as a chastening commentary on St. Paul's description of militant Christianity: Victorian hymnals were filled with Isaac Watts', Charles Wesley's, and others' famous injunctions to 'Soldiers of Christ' to arise and gird themselves for unflinching battle; Baring-Gould's famous 'Onward, Christian Soldiers' was written only two years before 'Dover Beach' was first published in 1867. All of these hymns assert that Christians fight heroically under divine leadership; and none trouble to name a particular antagonist. As Thomas Carlyle stated when putting the image to his own uses:

> Here on earth we are as soldiers . . . that understand not the plan of the campaign, and have no need to understand it; seeing well what is at our hand to be done. Let us do it like soldiers; with courage, with a heroic joy. 'Whatsoever thy hand findeth to do, do it with all thy might.'[4]

John Keble once observed when sounding his own 'war note' that 'our path of glory / By many a cloud is darken'd and unblest';[5] but no other hymns in this hortatory tradition even faintly hint such defeatism.

It was impossible for a young Victorian, especially a Rugbeian, not to fit himself into this heroic mould. Dr. Arnold often invoked it to exhort his students into battle for God's causes. He told his Sixth Formers to consider themselves 'like officers in the army or navy, whose want of moral courage would, indeed, be thought cowardice', and he reminded the entire School that

---

They are selected from many current in the century by their special similarity to those in 'Dover Beach', by their relevance to the predicament defined in this paper, by their appearing in the writings of men with whom Arnold was personally acquainted, and by their proximity to the few years within which Arnold wrote his poem.

[4] 'Characteristics', in *Critical and Miscellaneous Essays* (London, 1872), IV, 38.

[5] *The Christian Year* (Philadelphia, 1834), p. 205.

The infinite voice in the infinite sins and sufferings of millions . . . pro-
claims that the contest is raging round us; every idle moment is treason;
that not till the victory is gained may Christ's soldiers throw aside their
arms, and resign themselves to enjoyment and to rest.

Even at Oxford he told young men that /497/

the importance of not wasting the time still left to us may well be called
incalculable. When an army's last reserve has been brought into action,
every single soldier knows that he must do his duty to the utmost; that
if he cannot win the battle now, he must lose it. So if our existing nations
are the last reserve of the world, its fate may be said to be in their hands
—God's work on earth will be left undone if they do not do it.[6]

There were two ways by which, according to Dr. Arnold, the army's
duty is made known. One is by the evolving record of human history,
which Dr. Arnold interpreted as a cyclical progression in which
national states pass through distinct phases toward establishment of
ideal political and moral conditions, reaching toward the ultimate
form designed by Providence. Thucydidean Greece, he once observed,
had passed through the primitive phase, rule by a dogmatic aristocracy, to achieve rule by the rational and individualistic propertied
class. The third and ultimate stage should have been rule by numbers
in a democratic, spiritually unified community. But unfortunately the
propertied classes had failed to serve their own destiny by preparing
the masses of citizens for responsible rule. Instead they had served
their own acquisitive self-interest, allowing the masses to fall into
poverty and depravity while they embarked on the ruinous commercial wars that destroyed their civilization. England, Dr. Arnold
warned, was now approaching the same third stage; its masses were
wretched while its rulers were permitting only greater individual
competitiveness. Thus, Dr. Arnold warned, Thucydides speaks 'a wisdom more applicable to us politically than the wisdom of even our
own countrymen who lived in the middle ages.'[7]

---

[6] A. P. Stanley, *The Life and Correspondence of Thomas Arnold, D.D.* (London,
1844), I, 108; *Christian Life, its Course, its Hindrances, and its Helps: Sermons
Preached Mostly in the Chapel of Rugby School* (London, 1841), p. 102; and
Introductory Lectures on Modern History, seventh ed. (London, 1885), pp. 30 f.

[7] *The Miscellaneous Works of Thomas Arnold, D.D.* (London, 1874), p. 109. The
whole of Dr. Arnold's cyclical theory appears in an appendix to his Thucydides
reprinted in *Miscellaneous Works*, pp. 81–111 (cf. pp. 396 and 399). Lionel Trilling,
Matthew Arnold (New York, 1949), pp. 50–52, seems to overstress Vico's influence;
Dr. Arnold owed as much to Niebuhr, Müller, and apparently Guizot.

This historical vision gave an immediate, pressing relevance to the study of Thucydides at Rugby, imparting a sense of urgency to Dr. Arnold's program for present national reform. He was careful to provide his students with 'formulae' for reading ancient or modern history, 'what to look for in it, how to judge of it, and how to apply it';[8] and he argued continually that *laissez-faire* morality in the State together with outmoded sectarianism in the Church were now combining to thwart God's purposes for England, entry into the third stage of its social evolution, establishment of a democratic Christian community. A unified Church was an essential prerequisite to political reform, because only when men are united as a single Christian army can they avoid the fate described in 'Dover Beach', 'help one another, /498/ and not leave each man to fight his own fight alone'.[9] As the Rugbeian J. P. Gell wrote the Rugbeian Arthur Hugh Clough,

> It seems a proved point (by De Tocqueville and Guizot) that democracy must come on, that it is mere destruction except under a religious form, that in fact the most pure and effective form of Christianity is that of a religious democracy ('the spiritual man judgeth all things but himself is judged of none' = vox populi vox Dei) and consequently the happiness or misery of the world now depends on the speed of this pure form of Christianity not on the impossible attempt to check democracy. Now Clough let us turn radicals.[10]

Clough had already done so. Every Rugbeian could read in Thucydides' account of the disastrous night battle on the plains of Epipolae an image of the present moral condition of England, and an image of the future if they refused to serve God's purposes:

> The whole army now fell into utter disorder, and the perplexity was so great that from neither side could the particulars of the conflict be exactly ascertained. . . . The moon was bright, and they saw before them . . . the figures of one another, but were unable to distinguish with certainty who was friend or foe . . . no one knew which way to go . . . there was nothing but confusion.[11]

Arnoldians became dedicated Christian soldiers in order to avoid the fate of their Thucydidean predecessors.

---

[8] *Miscellaneous Works*, p. 360.

[9] *Life and Correspondence*, II, 66.

[10] *The Correspondence of Arthur Hugh Clough*, ed. F. L. Mulhauser (Oxford, 1957), I, 84, hereafter called *Correspondence*.

[11] *Thucydides*, trans. B. Jowett (Oxford, 1881), Bk. VII, Ch. 44, pp. 516 f.

God, Dr. Arnold taught them, would lead them to inevitable victory
if they listened to his commands in the infallible moral faculty given
them for that purpose, their conscience. This was their second guide.
They were 'bound to enforce the authority of the laws of conscience
and of God while . . . exposing the weakness and corruption of the
laws of man.'[12] It is not generally known that tremendous weight was
placed on this faculty by early Victorian theologians, with many un-
fortunate consequences. It may be sufficient to point out here that
faith in the sovereign authority and absolute infallibility of conscience
was encouraged by writers as diverse in their assumptions as Bishop
Joseph Butler and Samuel Taylor Coleridge, and by churchmen as
diverse in their theologies as Dr. Arnold, F. D. Maurice, six of the
seven contributors to *Essays and Reviews* (1860), John Henry Newman (especially before his conversion), and W. G. Ward.[13] /499/
Whether they considered conscience to be the moral faculty discussed
under various names by the Church fathers, the moral sense of the
Deists, or the Moral Reason defined by Kant, these men and many
others were convinced that each good man lives with a conscience
dictating God's will to him personally, and thus remains at all times
fully informed of his own moral responsibilities. They assumed that

---

[12] *Miscellaneous Works*, p. 117.

[13] Bishop Joseph Butler, *Sermons* (New York, 1844) pp. 25–31, 42, 67, 186, 271–
274; and *Analogy* (London, 1860), *passim*; cf. C. D. Broad, *Five Types of Ethical
Theory* (New York, 1930), and A. Duncan-Jones, *Butler's Moral Philosophy* (Ham-
mondsworth, 1952). For Coleridge see *Aids to Reflection* (Burlington, 1829), pp.
76–79, 115, 136–137; *The Table Talk and Omniana* (London, 1917), pp. 347, 396,
405–407, and *The Philosophical Lectures*, ed. K. Coburn (London, 1949), p. 364;
cf. C. R. Sanders, pp. 35–48. For Dr. Arnold see *Life and Correspondence*, II, 51–
52; *Christian Life*, pp. 97–98, 187, 235, 309; and *Sermons, Second Series* (London,
1834), pp. 142, 258, 385; cf. my *Arthur Hugh Clough's Formative Years* (Univ. of
Minnesota diss., 1959), pp. 28–33. See F. D. Maurice, *The Conscience: Lectures on
Casuistry Delivered in the University of Cambridge* (London, 1868), *passim*; and
see *Essays and Reviews* (London, 1860), pp. 5–6, 13, 18, 20, 42, 44–45, 51, 57, 82–83,
97, 99, 160, 162, 196, 267–269, 389, 411, and 413 (because they rested faith in this
faculty, they could view fallible features of Scripture calmly). For Newman see
*Sermons, Chiefly on the Theory of Religious Belief, Preached Before the Univer-
sity of Oxford* (London, 1843), pp. 19–22, 51, 55–56, 65–66, 134, 175; and *Apologia
Pro Vita Sua*, ed. D. Culler (Boston, 1956), p. 230; cf. F. James Kaiser, *The Concept of Conscience According to John Henry Newman* (Washington, D.C., 1958).
For Ward see *The Ideal of a Christian Church Considered in Comparison with
Existing Practice* (London, 1844), pp. 33–35, 260–262, 503–504, 589; cf. Wilfred
Ward, *William George Ward and the Oxford Movement* (London, 1889), pp. 73–76,
209, 250–256, 381, 422. I am presently engaged in separate study of this pervasive
concept in its Victorian manifestations, which have frequently been misunderstood.
It might seem to have fostered moral subjectivism; the curious fact remains that
none of its promulgators believed that it could, and so left themselves and their
followers peculiarly vulnerable.

conscience speaks with the same voice to all men, uniting them in knowledge of the duty, and that as the expression of God's voice the dictates of conscience carry higher authority than even Scripture or Church doctrine. The existence of conscience became for some the most unshakable evidence of a continuing providential government over human affairs. To Arnoldians who shared Dr. Arnold's historical vision, conscience was also the prime informant of God's will manifesting itself in social movements: as Clough wrote in an undergraduate essay 'Vox Populi Vox Dei', 'that Conscience which, says the poet, is to be "reverenced and obeyed / As God's most intimate presence in the Soul . . . " ' can always distinguish 'the real Want and Wish of Mankind' from 'fleeting phenomena' of casual opinion.[14] And mere faith in the heart-felt intimations of conscience was alone sufficient to validate them as God's word. 'He who believes his conscience to be God's law', said Dr. Arnold, 'by obeying it obeys God.'[15]

So, with minor variations, went the theory; the facts as young men of Matthew Arnold's generation found them were something else. One difficulty was in the assumption that all men necessarily agree about essential points of Church doctrine, unless they have deliberately perverted their moral faculty. Dr. Arnold assumed that this was the case with the Tractarians. If they claim that their doctrines are sanctioned by conscience, he said, /500/

> it can only be a conscience so blinded by wilful neglect of the highest truth, or so corrupted by the habitual indulgence of evil passion, that it rather aggravates than excuses the guilt of those whom it misleads.[16]

Newman in turn assumed that the same was true of modernists like Dr. Arnold. If they raise difficulties about the authority of Scripture, he said, it is 'for a plain reason,—they love sin':

> For ourselves, let us but obey God's voice in our hearts, and I will venture to say we shall have no doubts practically formidable about the truth of Scripture. Find out the man who strictly obeys the law within him, and yet is an unbeliever as regards the Bible, and then it will be time enough to consider all that variety of proof by which the truth of the Bible is confirmed to us.[17]

---

[14] Bodleian MS. Eng. Misc. d. 314, 28 November 1840.

[15] *Life and Correspondence*, II, 51.

[16] 'The Oxford Malignants and Dr. Hampden', *Edinburgh Review* LXIII (April, 1836), 239.

[17] *Parochial and Plain Sermons* (London, 1891), I, 200–201. Cf. Keble's similar statement in J. D. Coleridge, *The Life of John Keble* (Oxford, 1869), p. 582.

Yet when Clough departed from the reign of the 'great and good man' who had taught him at Rugby how to confront the Tractarian 'enemies' at Oxford, he found that the chief upholders of Tractarian doctrine were 'good and pious men'.[18] This was puzzling. Worse, he saw that Oxford was filled with good men righteously attempting to hound each other out of the Church, each convinced by his own conscience that his opponents were not merely in error, but in a state of sin, of deliberately refusing to listen to the truth within them. Newman saw fit to describe this theological warfare as 'a sort of night battle, where each fights for himself, and friend and foe stand together',[19] but his own convictions, like those of his antagonists, kept him in the struggle for many years. Clough became less certain that the Arnoldian party, or any parties to the controversy, were as enlightened about the creeds as they believed. As he wrote his sister about the apparent immorality of vicarious atonement, 'Until I know, I will wait . . .'. Even if all of Scripture should fall, he said, in essential matters of moral guidance 'belief in [God's] commands as written in our Conscience stand unshaken . . .'.[20] But he saw meanwhile that conscience does not provide all men with the same commands.

Francis Newman argued that theological confusion did not absolve Clough of his personal responsibilities as a Christian soldier. 'We have a battle to fight', he assured Clough, 'in truth, meekness and simplicity, /501/ to which the God of Truth will not refuse his blessing.'[21] But Clough had already seen the consequences when men mistake their zeal for their conscience and enter battle in darkness. So had his friend J. C. Shairp. In fact, during the 1840's Shairp realized that faith in conscience can render faith in formal religion unnecessary, and that responsible clergymen seemed implicitly in agreement with him: 'In the pulpit men talk of the dogma', he wrote Clough, '—in practice they hold to conscience and these two never pass one

---

[18] *Poems and Prose Remains of Arthur Hugh Clough* (London, 1869), I, 66; and *Correspondence*, I, 67.

[19] Quoted from *Sermons . . . Preached before the University of Oxford* by J. H. Cameron in 'The Night Battle: Newman and Empiricism', *Victorian Studies*, IV (December, 1960), 99. Julius Hare's *Vindication of Luther against his Recent English Assailants* (London, 1855), points out that the doctrine of infallible conscience preached by 'the new school of Sophists at Oxford' makes us 'not only still more prone to errour, but more presumptuous and headstrong in our errours', 'since every prejudice, every caprice . . . may be stampt with the authority of conscience'—pp. 129–130.

[20] *Correspondence*, I, 182.

[21] *Correspondence*, I, 190.

into the other.'[22] Unwilling to enter the ministry under such circumstances, and as unenlightened as Clough about the truth of Christian doctrine, he hoped finally that his difficulties were caused by a hidden but divinely ordained historical process working itself out independent of human effort:

> Sometimes I console myself with hoping that all this confusion and perplexity and suffering comes from Christianity's passing into its newer forms—while we like the man in Thucydides' night battle know not friend from foe.[23]

Denied light or power in matters of Church reform, Clough turned during the 1840's to serve the historical process on Dr. Arnold's other mandated battlefield, reform of commercial morality. Here, he assumed, conscience certainly speaks clearly, and he began preparing himself to become 'the Apostle of Anti-laissez-faire', a preacher to 'the soldiers, serving in the great industrial army of arts, commerce, and manufacture.'[24] In a public letter he denied that we should blindly 'trust to Providence' (as Carlyle had advised) and 'do our work in that state of life to which we are called.' The voice of conscience must always prevail over voices calling men into the market place:

> are we called to it? is it a providentially ordered duty? and is there not such a thing as running into temptation? Could any individual young man look his conscience steadily in the face and affirm, 'I am called to this profession, for in it I shall get most worldly profit.'[25]

But as he continued to explore the matter, he found that here too the orders were conflicting; and all he could finally advise, weakly, was that men somehow continue to be productive.

> I am not to regard myself as engaged in a petty warfare with all those for whom I work or who work for me . . . each man for himself and chance for us all; we are servants to each other, soldiers in a standing army . . . True it is, at first sight it seems otherwise: as in ancient warfare, so now in modern trade, each man is ordered to fight for himself. But the army is not therefore disbanded; we are still under orders . . .

---

[22] Bodleian MS. Letters, 227, 229, 230, and 232, listed in *Correspondence*, II, 627–628. Years later Shairp returned to the faith, no longer able to consider 'our weak moral instincts the criterion of all truth'—*Correspondence*, II, 377.

[23] *Correspondence*, I, 218.

[24] *Correspondence*, I, 130; and *Poems and Prose Remains*, I, 416.

[25] *The Balance*, January 23, 1846, p. 26.

whatever the tactics, /502/ whatever the commands, we are still to all
intents fellow soldiers, a single army engaged for the common good
against a single enemy, the earth, which we have to subdue . . .[26]

The laws of political economy seemed to work inexorably, with a
morality other than that supposedly dictated by God. Even on this
battlefield, as the unsteady ironies of his *Retrenchment* pamphlet
show, Claugh became uncertain of the light within him.[27]

The revolutions of 1848 gave him brief new hope. Like Matthew
Arnold's brother Thomas, Jr., he read events in Paris as long-with-
held evidence that historical movements are indeed guided by a
divine will working in human hearts and tending toward establishment of a democratic Kingdom of God. As Thomas Arnold, Jr., wrote
him, 'A God still lives then! Justice is still at the basis of things! . . .
God's will shall be done on earth as it in heaven!'[28] But when the
revolution in Paris ended with the commercial classes even more
firmly in control of the government than before, Clough was all the
more depressed. He began to suspect that all human affairs run their
course without divine guidance; as Matthew Arnold had to tell him,
'God bless you: there is a God, but he is not well-conceived of by
all.'[29] He resigned his Oxford Fellowship in order not to prejudice
his conscience against some future intimation of truth, but he now
found himself shorn of faith that God assuredly governs human
affairs either through conscience or through historical movements
interpreted by conscience. 'God's voice is of the heart', he wrote in
'Adam and Eve', but as he had to add:

> I do not say
> All voices, therefore, of the heart are God's;
> And to discern the Voice amidst the voices
> Is that hard task, my love, that we are born to[30]

---

[26] *The Balance*, March 20, 1846, p. 93.

[27] See especially the argument in *Poems and Prose Remains*, I, 284–288, where
Clough does not know whether to praise or condemn private spending for luxurious
purposes during unemployment and famine.

[28] Bodleian MS. Letter 306, listed in *Correspondence*, II, 629.

[29] *The Letters of Matthew Arnold to Arthur Hugh Clough*, ed. H. F. Lowry
(Oxford, 1932), p. 87. For Clough's view of events in Paris see *Correspondence*,
I, 203–213.

[30] *The Poems of Arthur Hugh Clough*, ed. H. F. Lowry, A. L. P. Norrington,
and F. L. Mulhauser (Oxford, 1951), p. 421; hereafter this edition is cited by page
references in the text. W. E. Houghton, in *The Poetry of Clough* (New Haven,
1963), pp. 80–91, has recently recognized that this poem is a study of various voices
in the Christian conscience. For its title (it is usually miscalled 'The Mystery of
the Fall') see my 'The 1951 Edition of Clough's *Poems*: a Critical Re-examination',
MP, LX (November, 1962), 122–123.

In this state of mind he wrote out his most detailed description of
the Christian soldier's predicament on a Thucydidean battlefield. In
The Bothie of Tober-na-vuolich (1848), his hero Philip Hewson is
identified as a young political radical who finds himself forced to
make a radical /503/ personal decision, whether or not to marry far
beneath his social station. As in much of Clough's work, great issues
lurk in this small moral problem. Philip's venerable tutor advises
against the match, employing a Carlylean argument:

> When the armies are set in array, and the battle beginning,
> Is it well that the soldier whose post is far to the leftward
> Say, I will go to the right, it is there I shall do best service?
> There is a great Field-Marshal, my friend, who arrays our battalions;
> Let us to Providence trust, and abide and work in our stations.

But in an extension of this image carrying it far past the narrative's
needs, Philip replies by defining the quandary confronting Clough
and others of his generation. Neither history nor conscience were
providing occasion and orders for battle:

> Where does Circumstance end, and Providence where begins it?
> What are we to resist, and what are we to be friends with?
> If there is battle, 'tis battle by night: I stand in the darkness,
> Here in the melee of men, Ionian and Dorian on both sides,
> Signal and password unknown; which is friend and which is foeman?
> Is it a friend? I doubt, though he speak with the voice of a brother.
> Still you are right, I suppose; you always are and will be;
> Though I mistrust the Field-Marshal, I bow to the duty of order.
> Yet is my feeling rather to ask, where *is* the battle?
> Yes, I could find in my heart to cry . . .
> O that the armies indeed were arrayed, O where is the battle!
> Neither battle I see, nor arraying, nor King in Israel,
> Only infinite jumble and mess and dislocation,
> Backed by a solemn appeal, 'For God's sake do not stir, there!'   (p. 170)

How Hewson resolved this problem we shall see shortly. Clough still
had to rely upon the moral instinct, since other authorities were
worse: yet that instinct remained silent, or when it spoke, spoke
wrongly as often as not.

Early in 1849 a letter from an old college friend reminded him that
for some the mandate to fight was still stronger than doubts about
whom to fight. C. E. Prichard told Clough that overweening trust in
the moral instincts, at the expense of the Church's teachings, had
led him astray. Prichard hoped that 'leaders' like Clough were still

somehow embattled on the same side as men in the ranks like himself. Yet he confessed that it was difficult to tell:

> I hope that many fight on the same side, whom the smoke of their own
> guns hides from one another. But I cannot hope it may continue so: else
> they may shoot one another and the enemy to be all the better.[31]

Clough could only agree. Moreover, Clough could acknowledge that
he himself still heard a mandate to keep fighting despite the confusion. As he wrote that summer in Rome, again reminded of his
reformist responsibilities /504/ by the sight of committed republicans
defending their city against the French.

> Say not the struggle nought availeth,
>   The labour and the wounds are vain,
> The enemy faints not, nor faileth,
>   And as things have been, things remain.
>
> If hopes were dupes, fears may be liars;
>   It may be, in yon smoke concealed,
> Your comrades chase e'en now the fliers,
>   And, but for you, possess the field. (p. 63)

Refusing to fight may have as important effect on the outcome as
fighting. Even so, the battle orders were unclear. When Clough raised
the issue once again several years later, it was with a heavy sense of
its difficulties:

> . . . there's no return, no looking back;
> Amidst the smoky tumult of this field
> Whereon, enlisted once, in arms we stand,
> Nor know, nor e'en remotely can divine
> The sense or purport or the probable end,
> One only guide to our blind work we keep,
> To obey orders, and to fight it out. (p. 298)

The most he could do as a 'poor trumpeter' was to 'bring the soldiers
from the wrong ground to the right', from concern with Church reform to concern with social reform, and then 'trust that they, at
least, will do something.'[32]

We shall see later where Matthew Arnold stood while witnessing
Clough and others losing themselves in the confusions of battle, but

---

[31] *Correspondence*, I, 236 and 239.
[32] *Poems and Prose Remains*, I, 305.

some conclusions can be suggested now. The Thucydidean image served some members of Arnold's generation to describe their confusion in a Church split into warring sects made all the more fanatical by their blind faith in conscience; and more narrowly it warned them that a nation given to commercial warfare despite the dictates of conscience must perish. The overlapping Christian soldier image defined for these men their obligation to fight on by whatever commanding voice they could hear, no matter how arbitrary. This strange warfare created many casualties, but faith in a Providence that governs human affairs through the conscience was finally one of them.

II. The Sea of Faith

The same men employed an alternative image to define the same predicament, one stressing the need for men to inundate themselves in the faith already described, to submit utterly to their conscience in the service of an historical providence. The calm sea contemplated by the speaker of 'Dover Beach' and then transformed into metaphor is obviously different in tenor from the 'estranging sea' found in other Arnold poems, and equally different /505/ from the stormy Sophoclean seas sometimes cited as sources for the poem. The sea invoked in 'Dover Beach' is characterized rather by rhythmic waves tossing figures at its edge, and by a slow tidal withdrawal leaving those figures stranded and exposed to the breath of the night wind. This too is reminiscent of statements by Dr. Arnold, Clough and others who claimed to know when the tide was full and when not. Arnold's image suggests that these men are cruelly self-deceived.

It is not stretching the metaphor to say that Dr. Arnold expected all of his disciples to submit themselves to the historical tide: he often used such language himself. In fact, when young men were turning away from service to moral and social progress, and instead taking up Tractarian concern with the recovery of pure dogma, Dr. Arnold wrote out a powerful extended simile defining their difficulty for them. In the preface to his sermons *Christian Life* (1841), he observed:

> . . . as the vessels in a harbour and in the open sea without it, may be seen swinging with the tide at the same moment in opposite directions; the ebb has begun in the roadstead, while it is not yet high water in the harbour; so one or more nations may be in advance of or behind the general tendency of their age, and from either cause may be moving in the opposite direction. Again, the tendency or movement in itself is liable to frequent interruptions, and short counter-movements: even

when the tide is coming in upon the shore, every wave retires after its advance; and he who follows incautiously the retreating waters, may be caught by some stronger billow, overwhelming again for an instant the spot which had just been left dry. A child standing by the sea shore for a few minutes, and watching this, as it seems, irregular advance and re- treat of the water, could not tell whether it was ebb or flood; and we, standing for a few years on the shore of time, can scarcely tell whether the particular movement which we witness is according to or against the general tendency of the whole period.[33]

Yet Dr. Arnold believed that anyone with a properly sensitive con- science can have no difficulty distinguishing false wave motions from the true tide. As he concluded this essay,

When we look at the condition of our country; at the poverty and wretchedness of so large a portion of the working classes; at the intel- lectual and moral evils . . . ; can any Christian doubt that here is the work for the church of Christ to do; that none else can do it . . . ? Look- ing upon the chaos around us, one power alone can reduce it into order, and fill it with light and life.[34]

When Clough took up his short-lived career as a social reformer, he became what he called a 'lacquey and flunkey' to this same 'Spirit of the /506/Age'.[35] Having submitted himself to the Zeitgeist he told others in a public letter on Corn Law repeal that the democratic tide was visibly advancing:

The advance of opinion on the subject reminds one of seashore impres- sions, when the tide, after slowly surmounting a steep inclination, at last commands a wide level space, and now not only rapidly pours over it in front, but, while we watch the moving masses before us, hems us in, unexpectedly, by innumerable little creeks in the rear. What a minute before was the safest dry land is already a part of the flood. Our refuge is transformed to our danger; nay, the very bank beneath our feet seems changing to a quicksand. The sooner we abandon it the better.[36]

---

[33] *Christian Life*, pp. v-vi. Carlyle once described mankind as 'but a floating speck in the illimitable ocean of the All . . . borne this way and that by its deep- swelling tides . . . of which what faintest chance is there that we should . . . ascertain the goings and comings'—'Characteristics', 22–23. This may describe a 'Sea of Faith' at the full, and so may have contributed vaguely to the image Arnold used in 'Dover Beach', but it is Dr. Arnold's image that invokes the problem of observation at the shore, of submission to known tides in order to help God's causes to fulfil themselves. Carlyle's sea is shoreless, implying that no such problem exists.

[34] *Christian Life*, lxv.
[35] *Correspondence*, I, 141.
[36] *The Balance*, January 23, 1846.

James Anthony Froude similarly found near floodtide 'a strong resolved and haughty democratic independence, heaving and rolling
under the chaff-spread surface.'[37] But Clough's faith in his ability
to discern such tides was short-lived. It produced some public letters,
a pamphlet, and many satirical poems designed to awaken conscience,
but the nation was still unmoved. He briefly thought the 1848 revolution a resurgent manifestation of the Spirit of the Age, but this too
failed, and with it his hopes.

Even so, in 1848 his lingering trust in '. . . a kind of impetus
within, / Whose sole credentials were that trust itself' (p. 434) en-
abled him to resolve Philip Hewson's problem of choice with a series
of tidal images, all of them referring to the strong inner feelings that
must finally be acted upon. That these originate outside the self is
established when Philip's 'great floods of feeling / Setting in daily'
from him to the heroine are finally felt by her in the same tidal form.
As she tells Philip, she fears only that the tide of his love will turn:

You are too strong, you see, Mr. Philip! Just like the sea there,
Which will come, through the straits and all between the mountains,
Forcing its great strong tide into every nook and inlet,
Getting far in, up the quiet stream of sweet inland water,
Sucking it up, and stopping it, turning it, driving it backward,
Quite preventing its own quiet running: and then, soon after,
Back it goes off, leaving weeds on the shore, and wrack and uncleanness: . . .
                                                                            (p. 161)

Better, she argues, never to be flooded at all. Yet, when she can feel
faith that Philip's tide of feeling will remain at the full, she descends
into it joyfully, as a stream into 'the great sea still before it; / There
deep in it, far, to carry, and lose in its bosom, / Waters that still from
their sources exhaustless are fain to be added' (p. 162).

Her faith does not seem, for a time, wholly justified. Philip is
troubled by his Tutor's Carlylean argument, and returns to his proper
duty with the issue still unsettled. Yet, the problem of finding the
battlefield and /507/ his place on it, and of his own mistrust of his
instinctive feelings, is finally resolved in a grand epic simile:

As at return of tide the total weight of ocean,
Drawn by moon and sun from Labrador and Greenland,
Set-in-amain, in the open space betwixt Mull and Scarba,
Heaving, swelling, spreading, the might of the mighty Atlantic;
There into cranny and slit of the rocky, cavernous bottom

---

[37] *The Nemesis of Faith* (London, 1849), p. 152.

> Settles down, and with dimples huge the smooth sea surface
> Eddies, coils, and whirls; by dangerous Corryvreckan:
> So in my soul of souls through its cells and secret recesses,
> Comes back, swelling and spreading, the old democratic fervour.   (p. 171)

So inundated with conviction, Philip casts off the dictates of prudence, marries, and carries his bride off to New Zealand, where with humble assurance he carries out the orders he has finally received, not to battle for the masses but more simply, to love and to subdue the earth by his own labor.

In similar fashion, the resurgence in 1849 of Clough's faith in an oncoming democratic tide was expressed in the tidal image that follows the battle image in 'Say Not the Struggle Nought Availeth', an image itself followed by another of light finally dawning over the darkened field:

> For while the tired waves, vainly breaking,
>   Seem here no painful inch to gain,
> Far back through creeks and inlets making
>   Comes, silent, flooding in, the main,
>
> And not by eastern windows only,
>   When daylight comes, comes in the light,
> In front the sun climbs slow, how slowly,
>   But westward, look, the land is bright.   (p. 63)

But again, Clough's hopes for the Roman republic proved misplaced, and as he was forced to conclude in 'Easter Day',

> For the whole world, and there is none but this,
> The whole world lies in wickedness:
>   Christ is not risen   (p. 478)

Thereafter he found faith in an inundating Spirit of the Age somewhat absurd. His 'Dipsychus' recovers from the belief that 'there is no God' by plunging anew into a sea of faith:

> Aha! come, come—great waters, roll!
> Accept me, take me, body and soul!—
>   Aha!   (p. 254)

But the Spirit who dominates that poem sardonically calls him back to the world as it is, for better or for worse: /508/

> But you—with this one bath, no doubt,
> Have solved all questions out and out.
> 'Tis Easter Day, and on the Lido
> Lo, Christ the Lord is risen indeed, O!   (p. 255)

Neither tides of conviction within nor tides of history without gave evidence of providential direction. Having been tossed several times on waves of self-generated hope he had mistaken for grand tidal movements, he abandoned the shores of faith altogether.

III.   Matthew Arnold's Commentary

Matthew Arnold's deep mistrust of submission to the reforming Spirit of the Age preached by his father is well known: he was too well aware of the difficulties frustrating any major social change, and too wary of changes he saw already occuring. He had early found it necessary to find his own course apart from his father's overwhelming moral imperatives, knowing perhaps that on a shared battlefield darkened by the dust of conflict a powerful father can unwittingly slay even his own son, as happened in 'Sohrab and Rustum'. Thus as Clough grew enthusiastic about various reform movements, Arnold tried rather to insulate himself from the 'din and whirl and brutality which envelop a movement of the masses.'[38] England was not ready, as he wrote in 'To a Republican Friend, 1848', to give over 'selfish occupation' and stand 'face to face with God'.[39] During the decade's various upheavals Arnold remained 'over-haunted by the pale thought, that, after all man's shiftings of posture, restat vivere,'[40] and he advised Clough often though in vain that one must face the world not with hopeful enthusiasm but with resignation. There were no great historical tides flowing: as he later wrote in *God and the Bible*, 'only when one is young . . . can one stand by the Sea of Time, and instead of listening to the solemn and rhythmical beat of its waves, choose to fill the air with one's own whoopings to start the echo.'[41]

Nor, though he knew of his father's faith in the sovereign moral faculty, could he trust it. 'Self Dependence' tells of an 'air born voice' finding a response 'in mine own heart' (p. 240) ; 'Meeting' mentions orders finally given in 'a God's tremendous voice' (p. 174) ; and as he wrote in 'Revolutions', 'The word, the order, which God meant should be. / —Ah, we shall know *that* well when it comes near' (p. 239). In *Culture and Anarchy* he placed great weight on what he called the '*humane* instinct', a secular conscience trained up only with great difficulty;[42] and in the poem /509/ originally entitled

---

[38] *The Letters of Matthew Arnold, 1848–1888*, ed. G. W. Russell (London, 1901), I, 4; cf. *The Letters of Matthew Arnold to Arthur Hugh Clough*, pp. 59 and 107.
[39] *The Poetical Works of Matthew Arnold*, ed. C. B. Tinker and H. F. Lowry (London, 1950), p. 7, the edition hereafter cited in the text.
[40] *The Letters of Matthew Arnold to Arthur Hugh Clough*, p. 68.
[41] (New York, 1883), p. XV.
[42] ed. J. Dover Wilson (Cambridge, 1950), p. 109.

'Anti-Desperation' he could advise: 'Sits there no judge in Heaven, our sin to see?— / More strictly, then, the inward judge obey!' (p. 171). But despite these traditional or wishful references to ultimate guidance, he knew that 'the word, the order' had not come, and that 'the inward judge' was easily confused with other voices in the self. As 'Self-Deception' says,

> . . . on earth we wander, groping, reeling;
> Powers stir in us, stir and disappear.
> Ah! and he, who placed our master feeling,
> Fail'd to place that master feeling clear   (p. 210)

Or as he pointed out in a tidal image in 'Isolation. To Marguerite':

> The heart can bind itself alone,
> And faith may oft be unreturned
> Self-sway'd our feelings ebb and swell—   (p. 180)

This being the case, he knew that what he called 'Hebraism, *strictness of conscience*', could only drive men more blindly into battle with each other.[43]

Lacking faith in historical tides or in the divine intimations of conscience, he could nevertheless view with saddened sympathy the plight of others who felt called on to battle for God's causes. As he said of 'The Lord's Messengers' who 'Gladly descend to the plain', these will end up 'Baffled, bewilder'd'; hardly one shall return 'Safe through the smoke of the fight, / Back to his Master again' (p. 216 f.). In 'Rugby Chapel' he described at length how an army originally marshalled by God was staggering leaderless and lost; men like his father must 'move through the ranks' and

> Strengthen the wavering line,
> Stablish, continue our march,
> On, to the bound of the waste,
> On, to the City of God.   (p. 215)

But as he knew it would be his father's voice that was calling orders, not the voice his father had trusted as God's.

Even so, there was a brief period during 1848 when he allowed hopeful feelings to overwhelm him, approached faith in a progressive

---

[43] *Ibid.*, p. 132; cf. pp. 143, 145, 148–150, and 156. For discussion and criticism of Arnold's later reliance on a moral instinct see W. Robbins, *The Ethical Idealism of Matthew Arnold* (London, 1959), pp. 167–171.

Zeitgeist, and considered joining others in battle. His fate was as 'Dover Beach' describes that of all who act so rashly. He and Clough found themselves agreeing about the 1848 revolution in Paris, as he said, 'like two lambs in a world of wolves'. Clough reported that Arnold was 'really heated to a very fervid enthusiasm' while the revolution was in progress, though 'sadly cynical again' after its failure. Having briefly abandoned his carefully balanced stoicism and suffered for it, Arnold was all the more bitter when friends lauded Clough's *Bothie*, a poem revealing to Arnold that Clough /510/ had not even yet learned his lesson. Better to dispense with 'them, the age, the poem, even you', he wrote Clough, than 'be sucked for an hour even into the Time Stream in which they and [you] plunge and bellow . . .' 'I took up Obermann', he told Clough, 'and refuged myself with him in his forest against your Zeitgeist.'[44] In 1849 he had to warn Clough again. 'For God's sake', he told him 'let us neither be fanatics nor yet chaff blown by the wind . . .'[45]

These two extremes defined the limits of Clough's and other would-be reformers' oscillations. The 'ignorant armies' in 'Dover Beach' fight on even in darkness, unaware that the commanding voices within them are not those of God; unguided, they are dangerous even to themselves. Similarly, their faith in the divinely flowing inundating tides of a progressive Zeitgeist, known by tides of feeling within, bring them to passive hopeful submission to the waves, but they are tossed back by events that prove to be merely transitory. Arnold held himself back from such shores, but Clough did not despite repeated disappointments. One can easily imagine Arnold writing 'Dover Beach' to Clough in the form of one more warning—even the lines 'Ah, love, let us be true / To one another' could have been addressed to the man he often called 'love', 'my love', and 'my well-known love' in affectionate letters about their plight in a chaotic world.[46]

But whether or not the poem was part of their continuing debate is not at issue here. More immediate are the implications of this study for an historical interpretation of the poem, a poem written when faith in conscience was most difficult to sustain, and composed of images with which that problem had already defined itself. In this context 'Dover Beach' proves to be not so much about the loss of faith—even of faith in conscience and history—as about the treacher-

---

[44] *The Letters of Matthew Arnold to Arthur Hugh Clough*, p. 95.

[45] *Ibid.*, p. 111.

[46] *Ibid.*, pp. 84, 86, 91, and 109; for the term 'love' see pp. 57, 59 (three times), 93 (three times), 95, and 106–107 (twice).

ous consequences of retaining some vestiges of it; it describes men living and acting as if faith were still justified, and so passively submitting their hopes or actively striving in a world that is already dark, random, and void of guidance or purpose. The speaker can hear the 'long withdrawing roar' of the tide, but the figures on the shore have no volition and so suffer accordingly. The soldiers should know that they are without unified command, but they fight on neverthless and so cause additional suffering. The faith 'Dover Beach' examines provided Arnold's contemporaries with an illusion of security and purpose, but an illusion worse than no faith at all. The desperate appeal on which the two images turn—'let us be true'—is not merely an appeal for faith in a faithless world, as is usually assumed (the lines are not, 'Ah, love, let us have faith / In one another'), but an appeal for *justified* faith, for a 'true' relationship, though most men maintain *unjustified* faith, are betrayed repeatedly, suffer and do not even know why. Arnold had seen his contemporaries eagerly expecting to be rewarded by light, by /511/ clear principles of action, but 'the true world for my love to live in', as he wrote Clough, 'is a general Torpor, with here and there a laughing or a crying Philosopher.'

By making a poem of the images with which other people had defined their predicament and defended their illusion, Arnold implicitly criticized them. But he also anticipated the Yeats who wrote, in 'The Nineteenth Century and After',

> Though the great song return no more
> There's keen delight in what we have:
> The rattle of pebbles on the shore
> Under the receding wave.

The art of the poem now subsumes even the suffering prefiguring it. And as with Yeats' poem, knowledge of its implicit allusions provides more profound pleasure in contemplating that art.

R. H. Super

The Dating of "Dover Beach"*

The publication of Professor Kenneth Allott's edition of Matthew Arnold's *Poems* (London, 1965) adds such weight to an opinion already bolstered by the authority of Professors C. B. Tinker and H. F. Lowry on the dating of "Dover Beach" that it is high time to call in question the nature of the evidence on which their conclusion is based. In Allott's words, the poem was "probably" composed in "late June 1851 (although not published until 1867)". The grounds for this opinion are (1) the existence of a leaf of Arnold's manuscript containing on one side a pencilled draft of lines 1-28, on the other side some penned notes about Empedocles that seem likely to have been made during the work on 'Empedocles on Etna" (published late in October, 1852,) and (2) the tradition that the visit to Dover alluded to in the poem took place in company with Arnold's bride shortly after their marriage on 10 June 1851. The fact that the pencilled manuscript ends "Ah love &c" is reasonably taken to indicate that the last nine lines of the poem, beginning with those words, were already in existence when the first twenty-eight lines were written down.

But the poem may indeed allude to the honeymoon visit to Dover without having been *written* then, and it may have been scribbled on the back of a leaf of notes of 1849–50 at *any* time thereafter (many a traveller must have had the experience of jotting notes on stationery picked up in a hotel a dozen years or more earlier than the jotting; old note-paper usually finds its way to the bottom of one's supply, not the top). Professors Tinker and Lowry say that "it is tempting to conjecture that the pencilled verses were made about the same

---

* Reprinted from *Notes and Queries*, n.s., XIV (February, 1967), 61–62, by permission of the journal and the author.

time as the notes on the life of Empedocles, [which] can hardly be later than 1850" (*T.L.S.*, 10 October 1935, p. 631). But conjecture is not evidence, and the temptation should be resisted; in the same sentence they quite properly call their deduction a "rash attempt" and they do not repeat it in their *Poetry of Arnold: A Commentary*. The dates that have most relevance are the dates of Arnold's books: early in December, 1854, be brought out his *Poems. Second Series* (dated 1855) without "Dover Beach"; his next dozen years saw only a third edition of the 1853 *Poems* in 1857 and *Merope*; then came *New Poems* in 1867, "Dover Beach" among them. Never thereafter was it omitted, /62/ not even from the volume of selections Arnold made from his own works in 1878. It is a very large assumption to suppose that Arnold would have omitted what has uniformly been regarded as one of his greatest poems from the collection of 1855 if it had been ready for publication then.[1]

How to date a poem that has been on the stocks for a long time may seem an open question; as we have seen, the conclusion of "Dover Beach" was probably written some time before the rest of the poem took form. But we do not know *when* even that part of the poem was written, nor do we know anything about the other stages of composition. Until some more convincing evidence about the dating is available, the poem must take its place *after* those published in the 1855 volume and all discussion of Arnold's poetry that assumes earlier composition is on shaky ground. Without making a judgment of the criteria he used, one can point out that Professor Warren Anderson finds Arnold's imagery and classical allusion in the main body of the poem more of a kind with Arnold's poems of the late than the early fifties (*Arnold and the Classical Tradition* [Ann Arbor, Michigan, 1965], pp. 69–70, 204).

---

[1] As Professor Allott remarks of "Philomela": "If written in 1851, [the poem] would probably have been included in [the volume of] 1852." By the same token, the dating of "Stanzas from the Grande Chartreuse" can be made reasonably precise: it was not among the poems published in December, 1854, but appeared in *Fraser's Magazine* at the beginning of April, 1855. The most reasonable assumption, then, is that it was not finished when the volume of poems went to the press.

Kenneth Allott

The Dating of "Dover Beach"*

I

Professor R. H. Super thinks (ccxii. 61–2) that the evidence for supposing Matthew Arnold's "Dover Beach" to have been written "probably late June 1851" is not only inconclusive, which is obvious, but so unsatisfactory that future editions of Arnold's poems with a chronological arrangement should place the piece "*after* those published in the 1855 volume" on the grounds that the most relevant dates in attempting to say when it was composed are "the date of Arnold's books". "Dover Beach" was first published in *New Poems* (1867), and the books with which we are concerned are Arnold's collections of poems from *Empedocles on Etna, and Other Poems* (1852) to the third edition of *Poems* (First Series) in 1857. Super holds that it is "a very large assumption" to suppose that Arnold would have omitted "Dover Beach" from *Poems. Second Series* (1855) if the poem had been completed by December 1854, but by the same logic "Dover Beach" could not have been completed before the publication of *Poems* (1857)—Arnold added one new poem to that collection (the poem later entitled "Isolation. To Marguerite") and could therefore have added "Dover Beach" if it had been ready for publication. (In 1855 there were two new poems, in 1857 there was one.) This is ultimately unimportant because Super's conclusion either in its original form or as corrected is invalid. It assumes that Arnold would not withhold a completed poem from his next collection to be published, and this assumption is false. We know that the poet wrote "Calais Sands" in August 1850, but he did not publish it until 1867. Again,

---

* Reprinted from *Notes and Queries*, n.s., XIV (October, 1967), 374–75, by permission of the journal.

"Isolation. To Marguerite" almost certainly belongs to 1849, but it was not included in a collection until 1857. Super's general rule, then, that a poem once completed would appear in Arnold's next collection allows of exceptions. Why Arnold delayed the publication of "Calais Sands", why he abbreviated "The River", and why he very probably held back for some years from the reading public "Isolation. To Marguerite", are matters for conjecture. It is conjecture, for example, that Arnold, who had married in June 1851, may have felt "Calais Sands" too personal and too intimate a revelation of his feelings for publication in 1852, but it is a conjecture that fits the facts and is not otherwise incongruous. Similarly, "Dover Beach" may have been withheld from publication in 1852 as too personal and also perhaps as a picture of the human situation too unorthodox and too "black" not to be distressing both to his wife and to some members of his own family. I repeat that here we are dealing in conjecture, but it is a fact that "Calais Sands" was withheld from publication in the same way that we must suppose "Dover Beach" to have been withheld if it was composed in 1851. It is clear that "the dates of Arnold's books" provide no firm evidence at all for the date of composition of "Dover Beach".

Is the dating "probably late June 1851" so unsatisfactory? In so far as Super is objecting to extravagant guesswork I applaud his scepticism and have no quarrel with him, but I believe that in this instance he undervalues the two pieces of independent evidence that he cites and disregards the evidence provided by the poem itself. The independent evidence is (1) that the pencilled draft of ll. 1–28 ending /375/ "Ah love &c" is found on one side of a sheet containing on its other side Arnold's notes on Empedocles from the introduction to Karsten's *Philosophorum Graecorum Veterum . . . Operum Reliquiae* ii (these notes belong to 1849–50), and (2) that there is a tradition, to use Super's words, "that the visit to Dover alluded to in the poem took place in company with Arnold's bride shortly after their marriage on 10 June 1851". It has been shown that Arnold did visit Dover in late June 1851—see my edition of *The Poems of Matthew Arnold* (1965), p. 240. Further, it is common ground between Super and myself that the last nine lines of the poem (ll. 29–37) were probably "already in existence when the first twenty-eight lines were written down". Indeed Super seems ready to accept that ll. 29–37 were probably written about the time of the Dover visit, but he argues that ll. 1–28 could have been composed "at *any* time thereafter" and implies that it is distinctly possible that they were written after an interval of several years. Now it is conceivable that this sheet of Arnold's notes was left lying about after the publication of "Empedocles of Etna" and providentially came to hand when he was inspired to recall his honeymoon visit to Dover a number of years after the event. It is conceivable, but unlikely. It is surely much more likely, weighing possibilities, that the sheet of notes was handy because Arnold was still working on his dramatic poem. In the same way it is psychologically more probable that Arnold should have written with such tender recall of the situation when his honeymoon visit was still fresh in his mind than that he should have done so somewhat mysteriously several years later when he was *bon père de famille* and a busy school-inspector who found it increasingly hard to write poetry. Does the poem itself not suggest to a candid reader in ll. 29–37 a man on the threshold of a new phase of his existence, and is it plausible, if these lines were written on or shortly after the honeymoon visit to Dover, that they should have remained so distinct in the writer's mind that he could finish his draft of ll. 1–28 "Ah love &c" after a lapse of years? Which explanation does less violence to our sense of what is likely to have happened? After weighing all the evidence, including the reminiscences in "Dover Beach" of Senancour and Sophocles, both of whom were certainly in Arnold's mind when he was working on "Empedocles on Etna", and also the interesting parallel between the "distant northern sea" (l. 20) and the "far northern strand" of "Stanzas from the Grande Chartreuse" (l. 30), a poem associated with Arnold's continental honeymoon in September 1851 and probably written mainly in 1852 (as I have argued elsewhere), I am forced to conclude that, although we do not *know* when "Dover Beach" was written, "probably late June 1851" is a sober and rational conjecture. It would be agreeable if conclusive evidence of the date of composition were one day to turn up. Meanwhile I can see nothing to connect the poem with the late 1850's. Until further evidence is discovered I think the provisional dating "probably late June 1851", which is supported by what evidence now exists, should stand.

John Racin

"Dover Beach" and the Structure of Meditation*

Few poems have received as much critical attention as Matthew Arnold's "Dover Beach."[1] Indeed one might resolve, as did one writer in these pages, never to read another account of the poem. Despite considerable diversity of interpretation, most readers have seen that the main subject of the poem concerns the withdrawal of the Sea of Faith, a subject that motivates the general tone of melancholy evident from the beginning of the poem. What has not been noted, however, is that for his subject Arnold used a formal structure which was popular in English poetry when the Sea of Faith was at the full. An attendant effect is a curious irony that some critics have felt but have been uable fully to account for, an effect partially created by Arnold's firm control of the logical structure of the poem contrasted with a conclusion which posits a joyless, loveless, dark, contingent world, a world threatened with collapse into chaos.

The logical structure of "Dover Beach" has as its exact parallel the tripartite structure employed in the meditative poems of Donne, Herbert, Vaughan, and other devotional poets of the 17th century. Working within the general requirements of the meditative structure, Arnold was able to underscore, by the very form he used, the extremely bleak ramifications of the loss of faith he describes.

Since Louis L. Martz's pioneering work on the meditation, the terms "composition," "analysis," and "colloquy," have become firmly

---

* This essay is to appear in *Victorian Poetry*, VIII (March, 1970) and is printed here in prepublication form by generous permission of the author and the editor of the journal. Students should cite the casebook when quoting from this article.

[1] It is a pleasure to acknowledge that the idea for this paper was stimulated through conversations on the poem with a colleague, Mrs. G. William Jaquiss.

established in the language of criticism.[2] The overall purpose of the meditation was "to excitate the will to holy affections and resolutions,"[3] and this purpose was to be achieved in three stages.

The meditation began with the composition of place or of similitude, or with a combination of the two. The former employed the memory, the latter the imagination. Both were powers of man's sensible soul governed by the sensibles or particulars of his experience.[4] These particulars were to invoke the passions or affections necessary to incline the will to "holy affections," the indispensable goal of the meditation. Donne's "I am a little world made cunningly" and his "Let man's soul be a sphere" exemplify composition by similitude, and the first six lines of Herbert's "Church Monuments" illustrate a typical composition of place.

The second stage of the meditation employed the cognitive faculty of the rational soul, the understanding. This movement from the purely sensory memory or imagination to the rational was a movement towards God, the supremely rational. In this stage, reason analyzed the significance of the sensory experience. The analysis demonstrated that the profoundest experience available to man becomes intelligible when reason performs its proper role. The analysis took many forms, but in general it may be described as the application of reason to experience in order to prove the intelligibility of faith: *intellego ut credam.* Further, this discovery of meaning was intended to stir the will, the appetitive power of the rational soul, to embrace the good as defined by reason.

The meditation concluded with the colloquy, generally a petition addressed to God, to Christ, to the soul, to an object of loving concern. In this way the meditation ended on a note of exalted fervor invoking the hope of salvation and a vision of the coming Apocalypse.

Thus the meditative structure (a microcosm, it was argued, of the Trinity) employed the imagination-memory, reason, and will, faculties which allowed the poet to imagine-remember, to understand, and to love God. Further, the structure was a paradigm for a Christian

---

[2] *The Poetry of Meditation*, New Haven: Yale University Press, 1954. I used the 2nd edition, 1962. For his discussion Martz drew mainly on the work of 17th century English poets. But he also demonstrated the influence of the meditation on Wordsworth, Hopkins, Emily Dickinson, Yeats, and T. S. Eliot.

[3] St. Francis de Sales, *A Treatise of the Love of God*, Douay, 1630. p. 325. Cited by Martz, p. 15.

[4] Perhaps the best short summary of the faculty psychology reflected in the meditation is the Preface to Nicholas Coeffeteau's *Tableau des passions humaines*, Paris, 1615. The work was translated into English by Edward Grimeston, *A Table of Humane Passions*, London, 1621.

view of history which interpreted human experience in relation to the coming Apocalypse, which was to end history.

The opening fourteen lines of "Dover Beach" combine the characteristics of place and similitude. The place, seen and heard, is incredibly attractive, as Yvor Winters wrote: "one of the finest passages in the century."[5] Yet the tone of dignified, controlled melancholy, "the eternal note of sadness," goes far beyond the motives implicit in the literal dimensions of the scene itself. However, the motive is clarified in the second part of the poem (ll. 15–28). Here we learn that the place is the primary similitude of the poem. The sea at full tide is a vehicle for that period in history when religious faith was at the full. The motive for the note of sadness is the poet's realization that the night scene, the full tide, etc., are subject to change, that the religious period of history in its fullness was on the threshold of a long, slow retreat into extinction.

Arnold's analysis, his application of reason to the opening scene, leads to a markedly different conclusion from that of the 17th century devotional poets. Sophocles found in the sound of the sea an archetypal pattern for the ebb and flow of human misery. "Ebb and flow" accurately adheres to the ancient Grecian idea of eternal recurrence, a recurrence made inevitable by cyclical time set in an eternal universe. Murray Krieger finds in this idea the key to the poem. He writes: ". . . the ebb and flow, retreat and advance, and the endless nature of these, are precisely what is needed to give Arnold the sense of eternal recurrence which characterizes the full meaning of the poem."[6] For Krieger, the image of tidal conflict is everlasting, we "feel the unprogressiveness of man's ever-repetitive circular history,"[7] and man's fate is "pitilessly bound by the inescapable circle."[8]

The full implications of endless "ebb and flow" are grim indeed; nevertheless such a theory of history would suggest the periodic return to eras of religious faith. Arnold, however, hears not the "ebb and flow," but only the long, withdrawing roar of the Sea of Faith. There is not the slightest hint in the entire poem that the Sea of Faith may be gathering its forces for a return. The development of thought within the poem indicates that time is linear, a concept which makes recurrence impossible. This point is quite important, for it makes the meaning of the poem far more tragic that Krieger's read-

---

[5] *The Forms of Discovery*, Denver: Alan Swallow, 1967. p. 184.

[6] " 'Dover Beach' and the Tragic Sense of Eternal Recurrence," *University of Kansas City Review*, XXIII (1956), 74.

[7] *Ibid.*, p. 78.

[8] *Ibid.*, p. 79.

ing will allow. It is, of course, literally true that tides retreat only to advance again. But Arnold's tides are not real tides, nor is his view of history the same as that of Sophocles.[9]

Arnold's view depends on the Hebraic-Christian assumptions that time is linear, that it exists within a universe that had a beginning *ex nihilo* and will have an end *ad nihilum*. Thus the past is irretrievable, and no repetition is possible. St. Augustine and Christian historians such as Orosius, Otto of Freising, and a host of others dwelt upon the blackness of the human state in such a universe. But they countered this condition with the promise of the Apocalypse. An eternity of light was to follow temporal blackness. Arnold's poem holds out no hope for any version of an apocalypse. As we shall see in his conclusion, it suggests quite the opposite. If the Sea of Faith is to return periodically, the tragic implications of the poem are lost, and it becomes "comic" in the medieval sense; *i. e.*, the prospect of a return to the folds of the "bright girdle furled" even for a time is a happy one.

In the second part of the poem, Arnold's analysis concludes that faith is no longer possible: for him *intellego ut non credam*. Except for his commitment to linear time, which makes recurrence impossible, Arnold does not attempt to explain why. The sea metaphor only suggests that human experience and belief are subject to vast, powerful forces beyond man's control. "The folds of a bright girdle furled" connotes the attractiveness of faith, but the connotations are severely bound by the rational explicitness of the analysis. Reason grants the past splendor of faith, but no more than that. We are reminded of Arnold's words: "I cannot conceal from myself the objection which really wounds and perplexes me from the religious side is that the service of reason is freezing to feeling, chilling to the religious moods; and feeling and the religious mood are eternally the deepest being of man, the ground of all joy and greatness for him."[10]

Arnold's colloquy, beginning with "Ah love, let us be true / To one another," sharply contrasts with the generalized analysis. The colloquy stirs initially a sense of intimacy and hope. As R. A. Forsyth points out: "It seems natural that in his personal efforts to re-establish an 'heroic' balance in his 'unpoetic' times, Arnold should be driven back on human love as the experience through which he would most likely

---

[9] For an excellent discussion of Arnold's view of history see R. A. Forsyth "The Contrasting Views of Arnold and Clough in the Context of Dr. Arnold's Historiography," *ELH*, XXXV (1968), 218–253.

[10] C. B. Tinker and H. F. Lowry, *The Poetry of Matthew Arnold: A Commentary*, London: Oxford University Press, 1950. p. 270.

resolve his sense of isolation and loneliness."[11] But the possibility of human love is not Arnold's resolution in "Dover Beach." Certainly the prospect of fidelity in love echoes, however faintly, the ecstatic tone of hope and love in the devotional poet's petition to God or Christ, a petition supported by the long tradition of the essential promise of Christianity. Arnold's poem invokes human love as a substitute for divine love, a substitute made necessary by the loss of faith, but his invocation is muted because his "love" makes no response, but remains passive and uncharacterized. So slight is "love's" role that Yvor Winters saw this love as offering "a solution so weak as to be an evasion of the problem posed."[12] But surely this "love" provides no solution at all, nor can one believe that Arnold meant it to. Immediately following his brief petition to "love," he turns our attention to the world. His characterization of the world rules out the possibility of fidelity in love:

> for the world, which seems
> To lie before us like a land of dreams,
> So various, so beautiful, so new,
> Hath really neither joy, nor love, nor light,
> Nor certitude, nor peace, nor help for pain.

Whereas the devotional poets asked for God's saving love in order to triumph over a world as dark, confused, and chaotic as Arnold's and had no doubts but that God's love was more powerful than the world, Arnold asks for human love in a context which makes the world's "triumph" and man's tragedy certain.

Arnold's closing lines are a prelude to disaster:

> And we are here as on a darkling plain
> Swept with confused alarms of struggle and flight,
> Where ignorant armies clash by night.

The vision may appall us, but it is the corollary of Arnold's analysis. A world without religious faith is doomed to destruction. As we have seen, the colloquy of the traditional meditation was to stimulate the will to "holy affections." Arnold's colloquy, the logical and rhetorical climax of the poem, leaves the will helpless to avert the coming catastrophe.

This study of the structure of "Dover Beach" helps to account for the pervasive irony of the poem. Arnold, using the rigorous structure

---

11 Forsyth, p. 234.
12 Winters, p. 184.

of the meditation, highlights the revolution in religious thought that took place in English history. His evocative Wordsworthian "place" contrasts with the explicitly Christian scenes, such as Christ's passion and Judgment Day, of the earlier tradition. His analysis grants the attractiveness of Christian faith, but argues its demise. His colloquy points not to the light of the Apocalypse, but to a darkening future of unrelieved terror to be climaxed by a fearful close.

On the basis of internal evidence alone, this study thus far argues that Arnold's use of the meditative tradition was deliberate. It remains to consider what external evidence exists. Arnold read St. François de Sales, who, as Martz has shown, was instrumental in defining the meditative process and exerted considerable influence on the English devotional poets.[13] More telling is Arnold's knowledge of George Herbert, about whom he wrote in *St. Paul and Protestantism*: "And surely it can hardly be denied that the more eminently and exactly Christian type of righteousness is the type exhibited by Church worthies like Herbert. . . ."[14] His note-books show that he read Izaak Walton's *Life of Herbert*[15] and that he read Herbert's *Country Parson*.[16] Even more suggestive is that by 1867 as a *terminus ad quem* he read, as he himself noted "G. Herbert's poems."[17] In his note-book he quoted from "The Church Porch," Herbert's introduction to *The Temple*, three times.[18] In his note books he also quoted from "The Elixir"[19] and in *Culture and Anarchy* from "The Size."[20]

This external evidence is by no means conclusive. Yet it does show that the religious devotion exhibited in Herbert's life and works could have suggested to Arnold Christian faith at the full. Further, it shows that there is nothing inherently improbable in the surmise that he knew the meditative structure and that he deliberately employed it for ironic effects. The stronger evidence is the structure of "Dover Beach" itself.

---

[13] Arnold owned a copy of *Esprit de St. Francois de Sales*, and quoted from it in his note-books. *The Note-books of Matthew Arnold*, ed. by H. F. Lowry, K. Young, and W. H. Dunn. London, 1952. p. 480.

[14] *The Complete Prose Works of Matthew Arnold*, ed. R. H. Super. Ann Arbor: University of Michigan Press, 1960–66. Vol. VI, p. 104.

[15] *Note-books*, p. 582.

[16] *Note-books*, p. 587.

[17] *Note-books*, p. 581.

[18] *Note-books*, pp. 68, 97, and 102.

[19] *Note-books*, p. 77.

[20] *Prose Works*, Vol. V, p. 169.

William Cadbury

Coming to Terms
with "Dover Beach"*†

The surprising thing about "Dover Beach" is that, like Matthew
Arnold himself, it is so cheerful despite the gloom of what it says.
At best, we should think, we might wryly come to terms with Arnold's
world by recognizing our bondage, as ignorant armies on the darkling
plain, and in that recognition enduring if not prevailing. But I think
that "Dover Beach" incites to more than wry satisfaction. As well
as a progression from illusory freedom towards accepted bondage,
there is in the poem a more important progression from sentimental
attachments towards Promethean freedom and Promethean rewards.
We seem to escape from a stultifying room to the darkling plain on
which the tensions of introspection are resolved in action; the poem
makes us accept bondage among the ignorant armies as a kind of
release. I think that we accept the final struggle at least as wholeheartedly as we accept the commitment of the narrator of "Maud"
to the Crimean War, and for very similar reasons.

Like "Maud," "Dover Beach" provides a symbol of the Victorian
dilemma. Each poem presents a version of reality which does justice
both to a sense of intellectual despair and to a hope that human action may avail after all. And in each, this double sense is created
generically, each poem presents a narrator whose feelings progress
in the course of the poem in such a way that the total design is of
his mind in its seeing and working. We go with him through the
process of attacking problems, and we come with him in the end to

* Reprinted from *Criticism*, VIII (Spring, 1966), 126–38, by permission of the
journal.

† I am indebted to the University of Oregon Office of Scientific and Scholarly
Research for financial support of this study.

a way out of his impasse, a way which is acceptable to the feelings and which lets the intellect take its bleak way unmolested but ignored.[1]

The two progressions, towards bondage and towards freedom, are different plots, which we may call "action" and "thought." Each has a different locus in the total world which the poem makes up: the /127/ locus of the action is the narrator, and that of the thought is the external world. The action is the progression of the narrator's motives, his attempts to say what he has to say and do what he wishes to do. The thought is the progression of descriptions of the external world. Though both plots are contained in the same words, we perceive them at different times, in the different organizations we make of the poem as we read it or think about it.[2]

The action of "Dover Beach" is the narrator's relation of his poem, with its changes of subject, its rises and falls, its turns to and from his companion; it is what the narrator *does*, the ways in which he copes with his world. The thought is what the narrator *says* about his landscape and its significance. Of course this thought only exists for us through the narrator; it is the result and sign of his feeling. What the narrator describes, however, carries for us feeling of its own, particularly in the sequence of images which seem to detach themselves from him, to be a self-contained design which we perceive without much concern for a designer. We can respond to what the narrator talks about differently from the ways in which he responds, and so we can understand what he copes with, as well as the ways in which he copes.

The narrator goes through a sequence of feelings, then, which we accept or reject, and differently at different stages; this is his action. But he also talks about something, and we respond to what he talks

---

[1] "Genre is determined by the conditions established between the poet and his public." Northrop Frye, *Anatomy of Criticism* (Princeton, 1957), p. 247. The analysis of literature by pregeneric forms is demonstrated throughout the third essay of *Anatomy*. This paper attempts to determine the relationship between pregeneric form and genre in "Dover Beach."

[2] In making sense of a poem, the reader "oscillates" between action and thought. They are among those "systems of contradiction in which temporary acceptance of one pole promotes preference for the other and vice versa" and in which the "time characteristic is important." Gregory Bateson, "Information and Codification: A Philosophical Approach," in Jurgen Ruesch and Gregory Bateson, *Communication* (New York, 1951), p. 196. I think that such distinctions as this of time in codification are vital, if we are to avoid what I take to be the danger of depending on a "magical" power of poetry to be two things at once. See, for instance, Murray Krieger, *A Window to Criticism* (Princeton, 1964), for the argument that poetry depends on "miracle."

about not only differently at different stages, but differently from him; this independent sequence is the thought.

I think that this essentially generic distinction between thought and action allows us to reach specification of the four pregeneric forms in structural terms: if thought and action support each other, then we are totally involved, and we accept the narrator's character as fully in tune with his world. This relation between thought and action determines the forms of romance and irony—for the first, we might educe Arnold's "A Summer Night," and for the second "The Rubáiyát." In each the narrator's final feeling is properly adjusted /128/ to what his thought, his presentation of the world, has implied, and he acts on right knowledge of that implication. In "The Rubáiyát" the narrator accepts his bondage, whereas in "A Summer Night" the narrator achieves freedom—but in both, the world presented allows and demands just that action.

But if action and thought are at odds, then our feeling for the narrator clashes with the feeling created by his thought. We see that his action is not adjusted to his world or what it should allow, and that he acts in ways which the implications of his picture of the world should deny. And here belong comedy and tragedy. If we find the narrator's character "better" than the implications of the thought allow character to be—if the narrator proves his worth in doing what he does, but claims that the world is one in which worth is impossible —we have tragedy. If he proves himself "worse" than the implications of the thought—if he seems imperfectly to deserve the good fortune which comes to him and yet has claimed and proved a benign world— we then have comedy. For comedy, we can claim Patmore's "Love at Large" of Browning's "Count Gismond"; for tragedy, "Maud" or "Empedocles on Etna." In romance and irony, then, the point is the sum of thought and action; in tragedy and comedy, the point is the difference between them.

To turn from theory to the poem "Dover Beach," the question, as I see it, is whether the poem is tragedy or irony. Does it present a sinking to darkness without benefit of extended wings, a direct statement about the drying up of the Sea of Faith? Or does it show a fortunate fall, a transformation of mankind from pebbles into soldiers? By my way of putting the question I imply my answer, but we must go through the levels of action and thought to document the case.[3]

---

[3] Mr. Krieger, in his able explication of the poem in " 'Dover Beach' and the Tragic Sense of Eternal Recurrence," *UKCR*, XXIII (1956), 73–9, finds, as I do, that the poem is a tragedy. But as his title implies, he finds that the tragic sense

The action of "Dover Beach" is the sequence of the narrator's attempts to find warrant in nature for communion with his love. /129/ Throughout the poem he tries to let nature take the initiative in proving love and communion, when nature's initiative can be made to support what he feels to be properly human feeling. But he accepts initiative for himself too, when nature's lessons seem to deny his aims. If we are not "In Harmony with Nature," he comes to feel, than we must "pass her" or "rest her slave."

At first the warrant he seeks seems easily obtained. As he stands at his window, nature lies before him, peaceful under the moon as in so many of Arnold's poems' beginnings. And the sense of peace, instilled by the scene, inspires him to share the sight with another; he calls to his love to join him in the pleasure which the whole scene may give—"Come to the window, sweet is the night-air!" But to the sense of sight has been added the sense of smell. And with this greater involvement, he becomes aware of another sensation which impinges upon him, but which his moonstruck sight had ignored. This is the sense of hearing, and it presents a proof of conflict which must be taken account of, and which was not apparent to the single viewer.[4] A man alone may, as in "In Utrumque Paratus," delude himself into a sense of symbiosis; but human contact creates an awareness which implies that nature has her initiatives too, and that she is in a condition of strife which may be the necessary image of human contact. When the narrator shares the scene, he finds it through his companion's ears—"you hear"—and the sound implies a strife which is far from what he wished to prove. Nature does not just lie there, blessing observers with tranquillity. Like men, it acts, and the acting implies men's subservience to the waves.

With full inspection of the scene, then, initiative is lost. Nature had seemed to imply companionship in detached observation, but that observation led to knowledge of the long "line of spray" which im-

---

lies in the fact that "the doom man carries with him he carries only to assert with it his eternal recurrence" (p. 77). I take the tragic sense to come rather from the narrator's insistence on the closest possible perspective on the scene, which denies recurrence and assures value. And I take this insistence on reduced perspective despite the pressure of thought to be the equivalent of the "moral grandeur" the lack of which, according to Wendell Stacy Johnson, prevents the attainment of tragedy in "Dover Beach." *The Voices of Matthew Arnold* (New Haven, 1961), p. 92. Adequate classification should come from analysis of structure, however, not from detection of qualities.

[4] Many commentators emphasize the distinction between images of sight and sound in "Dover Beach." See Krieger, "Eternal Recurrence"; Frederick A. Pottle, *The Explicator*, II (April 1944), item 45; Rodney Delesanta, *The Explicator*, XVIII (October 1959), item 7.

plies that nature's captives are not detached at all, but very much involved. In the couple's awareness of nature through each other was found denial of the communion which nature had seemed to imply. Painting has given way to music ("cadence," "tone"), stasis to sequence, eternity to time.[5] Looking at a passive natural scene has /130/ changed to listening to an active one, and the initiative has moved from observer to observed.

Awareness of nature's action having been thrust upon him in the sound of the waves, the narrator tries a way out of his impasse through an action of his own. He turns, as men and chickens will, to an auctoritee. From the turmoils of the events of time man makes the intellectual security of the acts of history, and so Sophocles is called in to prove continuity, communion across the ages if it is not available across the room. As Sophocles "Heard it on the Ægæan" the sound "brought / Into his mind" a thought. Nature's initiative, the sound, also acted upon the passive Sophocles, but Sophocles regained initiative through the act of thinking, and so may we; through the sense of oneness with Sophocles the narrator's initiative may be regained. Sophocles' perception of "the turbid ebb and flow of human misery" is certainly disheartening, but to be one in situation and in image-making with him "Who saw life steadily and saw it whole" gives confidence which enables the narrator's activity again, and therefore allows him to regain control—"we/Find also in the sound a thought." It is not the thought which had been thrust upon the narrator by the sense of hearing, but a new thought which demonstrates an active attempt to make sense of nature. The very act of finding a thought can undercut even Sophoclean gloom.

The new thought belongs to the couple, not just to the narrator, and so it is more appropriate to the narrator's initial goal; it is now "we" who find, not "I." But we know that the discovery of the new thought, coming as it does under the aegis of Sophocles and history, is an insufficient control over nature, whose roar, after all, remains. For a communion validated from within has been substituted one validated from without, from Sophocles. The intellect, in short, has done duty for the feelings. Since we know it is in our power to impose a sense of continuity on events through the arrangements of the intellect, we know that we are part of history, which is entirely

---

[5] Mr. Krieger takes the movement from sight to sound to be from time to eternity. Since I think that what is *seen* in the poem is invariably static, and what is *heard* is always evidence of process in the world, I cannot agree that sound permits us "to break free of the relentless clutch of the present occasion to wander relaxedly up and down the immensities of time" ("Eternal Recurrence," p. 76).

human, "the outward expression of thoughts" of Sophocles and of ourselves. But we know too that we are in time, in nature. We cannot use the sense of history to explain nature, since "nature has no history." It "presents us with a series of *events*, but history is not history unless it presents us with a series of *acts*. . . . There is no history except the /131/ history of human life, . . . not merely as life, but as rational life, the life of thinking beings."[6] The narrator's physical situation consistently implies that he must take account not only of Sophocles and of other humans, but also of his relationship to the insentient and unhistorical nature which he faces. It remains necessary for him to *act* in time, to make time into history through the externalization of his own thought. And he must make his history with his companion, who suffers the same subjugation to the events of time as the narrator himself, and not with Sophocles, whose kinship is only an intellectual construction.

With the satisfaction of control through the historical sense fresh in his mind, the narrator attempts to capture the scene before him through the intellectual creation of a history which will explain it. The portrait of a lesser illusion, the explanation of nature as a "Sea of Faith," begins the second half as the portrait of a greater illusion began the first half. The sequence which led to impasse and its resolution begins again, but this time the narrator presents it as a construction of the mind, not of the senses. To create the little allegory of the Sea of Faith is to take initiative again, to construct a conceptual parallel to the observed, estranging sea. History's replacement of time allows reflection to replace pure feeling. But we know that it will be lost effort, for the narrator's initiating motive was *not* reflection but feeling, communion. It is not acquiescence in historical gloom that he wishes, but validation of his state through the sense of a benevolent nature.

Pleasure again comes from a visual image, but visual images by now are known to be untrustworthy, and therefore the narrator's description here is by symbol and simile, not by the painterly directness of the opening image. Again he finds, however, that the honest inspection of the image requires rejection of its illusion. For this honest narrator the visual image of the Sea of Faith must give way to an image of hearing (nature's initiative again), and Sophocles' example is lost. This time, worse yet, hearing replaces sight instead of being added to it; moreover, the companion who was first gained is lost. "Now I only

---

[6] R. G. Collingwood, *The Idea of History* (New York, 1956; first published 1946), pp. 114–15.

hear"—I hear and that is all; and I hear by myself.[7] Nature takes
back her initiative, no matter how we try her. /132/

As he must in such a condition, then, the narrator turns from nature, back to the one possiblity for involvement which was excluded
from the recapitulation of the opening sequence. We remember that
at first his vision was a sharing—"Come," "you hear"; "we find." The
attempt to make solitary sense of his sequence of thoughts has led
to impasse—"I only hear." And so, the historicity of nature rejected,
he takes the only initiative left and turns back—"Ah , love, let us be
true to one another!" There is a possibility of salvation, of breaking
the impasse, if nature can be once more inspected from a specifically
human point of view with all illusions gone.

After the turn to the companion which proves initiative once again,
the narrator sums up what he has found to be unsatisfactory in "the
world"; it "seems" good, but it "hath" no good things in it. With
this simple but terrifying intellectual contrast of seeming and being
made plain, the operation of the intellect in these lines can again give
way to feeling, proved by the transmutation of thought into an
adequate image. The final lines create an image which is the consequence of reflection, not its cause; the image makes sense of the
world and the human condition without the illusion of the sea of
faith. Although the lines state despair and detachment from nature,
they present the very unity between observers and world which was
sought all along, but which only now gives the warrant for true
feeling. Instead of presenting himself as a detached observer from
a window, or as a singly meditating man creating the intellectual sense
of history, now the narrator accepts the fact that "we are here."
"Let us be" has become "we are"; observation of the world has
become participation in it, and the final and justifying initiative is
gained, not through the creation of illusion, but through the acceptance of reality.

In the final image we have sight once more, but now sight true
and not illusory. While the ending of the darkling plain is like the
symbolic turns we expect from Arnold at the ends of poems—the
description of the Oxus in "Sohrab and Rustum," the Tyrian trader
in "The Scholar-Gypsy"—it is not so much a shift in perspective
which assures us of what has gone before, as it is a reversal of expec-

---

[7] In the first version of the poem, the phrase ran "we only hear"; "I" is written
above, and is clearly a later change. C. B. Tinker and H. F. Lowry, *The Poetry
of Matthew Arnold: A Commentary* (London, 1940), p. 174.

tations which amounts to the narrator's achievement of truth and assertion of freedom.[8] /133/

The action of the poem, then, is a set of changes: from description of nature to involvement in it; from observation with a friend to dependence on the friend; from the attempt to capture something outside the self to acceptance of being captured. What looked like the security of faith was really bondage to illusion, and what looks at the end of the poem like helpless blindness of the darkling plain is really the tempered freedom of reality. The love to which the narrator turns is not so sad as Trilling suggests, I think;[9] it has the effect of an unveiling, as the turning from window to girl has the effect of acceptance of the human condition. The value of love becomes apparent only when it is clear that what is outside, the seemingly tranquil sea, is an illusion which in effect prevents love by diverting our attention from the human. We must be "true to one another" because there is no Sophoclean cycle or Medieval assurance to give value; but to find that these were illusions makes fully human love possible. If this be standing between two worlds, why we can truly make the most of it.

The action is, then, in brief, the narrator's acceptance of nature's eddying forms, which replaces his initial trust in the vision from the false security of the window. In his perceptions, he moves into nature, away from the falsely superior position in which "Thin, thin the pleasant human noises grow, / And faint the city gleams," in the similar imagery of "In Utrumque Paratus." The thought which is plaited with the action, on the other hand, is the reported and imagistically

---

[8] There is a long controversy on the appropriateness of the change from sea to land imagery. Mr. Pottle, for instance, disagrees with the reading of J. P. Kirby, *The Explicator*, I (April 1943), item 42, and claims that the symbolism is discontinuous, a "shift in point of view." Gene Montague, *The Explicator*, XVIII (November 1959), item 15, claims that the final image is a "shift from abstractness to concreteness," and is "organic," "Arnold's comment converted into metaphor." W. S. Johnson finds, on the other hand, a progression from "the wholly literal to the wholly metaphorical, from small to large abstractions" (*Voices*, p. 93), but agrees with Kirby and Montague that the "symbolic setting . . . is transformed," not just altered (p. 92). I think that the effect of the transformation is to call attention to the man transforming, to the character of the narrator displayed in the reversal. He suddenly perceives things in a new way, and I think that neither new nor old is the more abstract.

[9] *Matthew Arnold* (New York, 1955; first published 1939), p. 117. E. D. H. Johnson comes closer, I think, when he finds in "The Buried Life" and "Dover Beach" a "most strange and unexpected reversal of the sentiments" of the Marguerite poems, which prove the "failure to get outside the limitations of self through love." *The Alien Vision of Victorian Poetry* (Princeton, 1952), p. 160.

carried movement of nature away from man, the retreat of meaning which leaves us only the darkling plain. For what we have described as the action of the poem is our own perception of the narrator's achievement, and one he does not share. He is concerned not with the fact /134/ of his describing, but with what he describes. And he thinks that his poem *is* only the progression of its thought, the series of organizations which he is forced to make of his world. These move from illusory quiet, to perception of underlying struggle, and finally to entire gloom.

As the poem begins, the "light / Gleams and is gone" from the French coast. And though "the cliffs of England stand" reassuringly "out in the tranquil bay," of course it is a sad illusion. The proper image of the poem's thought is not the object of sight, the "moon-blanch'd land" which reminds us of "A Summer Night" and the landscape beyond the window of the sleeping children in "Tristram and Iseult." It is rather the pebbles flung by the waves. As imagery of sight and hearing characterized the action of the poem, and corresponded to the narrator's changes of feeling as he gained and lost initiative in his struggle to comprehend nature, so the image of the tossed pebbles characterizes the poem's thought, and corresponds to the various stages of feeling proper to the narrator's description of the world around him.

The pebbles, variously disturbing in the various ways the narrator perceives them, appear first as the element of disquiet which disturbs the pleasing unity of the scene conjured up for his love. Between fair-lying moonlit straits and moon-blanched land, wandering perhaps between two worlds, the pebbles are drawn and flung, first to the sea and then to the land; man's condition, it is implied, is to be alter-nately with one and the other, a condition even more powerless, more suffering in sadness, than that of Empedocles' "wind-borne, mirroring soul."

In the next appearance of this image complex, the "roar" which Sophocles heard is, as we would expect, more consoling. For it is not man's total condition which Sophocles deduces from the ocean's roar, but only the alternations of misery, so that we may be aware that misery ebbs and flows—sometimes there is less misery and some-times more, whereas the pebbles *always* suffered. But the images which carry thought move and change in accordance with the sug-gestions of the thought they describe, just as the images which carry action move in accordance with the strategies of their agent, the nar-rator. We have come to a distinction between the immediately per-ceptible waves which toss pebbles, and the larger, more ancient rise and fall of the roar of human misery. And this distinction leads to a further refinement of the image, which splits the difference in terms of time (as the Christian Sea of Faith stands between Sophocles and Arnold), but which abstracts the good, and the good only, from the possibilities /135/ which the image contains. Sophocles' somber analysis of the sea's roar, suggesting more the alternations of tides than waves, allows a consideration of tides alone; and tides may be high for a while, whereas waves may only rapidly come and go. The high-water mark of the poem's thought is reached through contemplation of the large view made possible by, but different from, Sophocles' large view of human misery. The narrator's modern fever can be allayed by the example of the dignity of the Sophoclean world.

The "thought" which "we find" is different from Sophocles' (since we are in a different place), but allegorical and sonorous where the first thought had to be immediate and tremulous. Waves, pebbles, and tides disappear, and "The Sea of Faith" is for the moment contemplated "at the full." Once we have forgotten the pebbles which prove man's helpless plight, we may find sea and land tranquil, the sea "furl'd" and protecting land "like the folds of a bright girdle," or like the sails which the image-within-an-image implies, furled round their mast. Though sea and earth are different, the relationship is not of enmity but of concord; the sea lets man know his place and its worth, and it is therefore beautiful.

While this image is as reassuring as the image to which it is parallel in the opening of the poem, this one, like that, contains the seeds of its decay. While waves may suggest tides and so allow a reduction of perspective in which we contemplate only the period in which a tide is high, the consequence must be the realization that tides don't stay up. For accurate specification of the modern human condition, we must reduce perspective still more.

The only sea-movement of importance has become the tide which Sophocles suggested. But when we look more closely at our part in the tide's general movement, we find that our share of its rise and fall is only the fall. For purposes of explaining the modern lot, the tide's return is unimaginably distant. Nature and God disappear together, "to the breath of the night-wind," and leave man without even the consolation of being tumbled by forces more powerful than he. As the tide "roars," "withdrawing" and "retreating" "down the vast edges drear . . . of the world," it leaves us exposed. We see ourselves as the "naked shingles" which have no ebb and flow, no contact with anything but each other, and no hope for anything externally caused—"sadness," "misery," or "faith." The thought of "Dover

Beach," at this point, simply adds up to Arnold's characteristic awareness that the finding of man's unity with nature, for good or ill, is
/136/ illusory. As Empedocles says, "we are strangers here; the world
is from of old."

From this point of view, the turn to the woman which follows *is*
the agonized response to nature's counsel of despair, a second-best
alternative to the oneness with nature which the narrator had thought
to find as warrant for human feeling. The analysis of the world in
its seeming and its reality then spells out the significance of the
images which have gone before. Each item of the catalogue of woes
now spoken had been designed as a part of the narrator's action when
creating images, by which he had tried to forestall just this recognition in which images no longer avail as they work themselves out in
utter gloom.

But we must not take the gloom of the catalogue to be the
"thought" of the poem in any but the technical sense we have established. Mrs. Langer points out that "In literature, the words 'no,'
'not,' 'never,' etc., occur freely; but what they deny is thereby created.
In poetry there is no negation, but only contrast."[10] When the narrator of "Dover Beach" spells out the qualities for which he has been
searching and denies each one, the qualities are raised in our minds
as he denies them. Aspirations, the visions of perfection he has
created, are set against the truth to which the images themselves
have impelled us.

The narrator specifies that the "land of dreams" which "seems /
To lie before us" has three attributes of seeming—it is "various,"
"beautiful," and "new." These attributes should prove three qualities
inherent in the world, "joy," "love," and "light." And these qualities
should provide three consequences to man, "certitude," "peace," and
"help for pain." But attributes, qualities, and consequences are all,
he says, false. And the contrasts between what might be and what
is not, the thoughts denied and created at the same time, indicate the
thought of the poem: that man can imagine the good but not feel it,
and that all his strategies, if honestly pursued, emerge in a recognition
of the hopelessness of thought and of the world which it organizes.

But recognition in literary structures usually contains the impulse
to a reversal. And the glory of "Dover Beach," the quality of cheer
for which we are looking, lies in its rejection of naked thought for
the human blend of thought and action in which feeling is most per-
fectly rendered. In the resolution of the poem the images which had
led to recognition are reworked. "We are here" proves acceptance

---

[10] *Feeling and Form* (London, 1953), p. 243.

of the nadir to which the images and their thought have brought the /137/ narrator. And his action then is to create an image which will fit, he thinks, the new knowledge. As thought, the new image of the darkling plain *is* accurate. The principle of variety and joy becomes confusion and flight where certitude is impossible; the principle of beauty and love becomes a clash of armies, which is certainly the opposite of peace. And "light" becomes the darkling plain, where alarms are heard, where mental clarity is seen to be ignorance, and where the reassuring temporality of "tonight" in the first line of the poem becomes the universal "by night" of the last. None of these presents much help for pain. Sight has become hearing, peace war, love armed and ignorant.

The final image is adequate transmission of the thought of the catalogue. But the narrator's action in creating this image implies something rather different from what the thought claims. The final image of the darkling plain is, on the level of thought, a reworking of the recognition stated in the catalogue of woes; that is, it is something new, an image which denies the implications of the poem's previous imagery. On the level of action, however, it is not new at all, but a fulfillment of the series of strategies in which the narrator had sought to encompass the world and his place in it. The very act of presenting it as a conclusion proves his integrity and the worth of his vision as well.

Since nature is admitted to have withdrawn from man, man can only be felt to have been left naked to a hostile sky. Yet the roar of pebbles which was heard at first, and on which all the subsequent imagistic changes have been rung, was not false, though it seemed at first so alien to the peace implied by the view from the window. Without the delusions of sight, light, peace, and joy, the narrator's perspective on the pebbles can change once more. Perspective was reduced, as waves became tides, and tides the withdrawing flow of faith; it was reduced as the line of pebbles became the road of human misery, and then naked shingles. Now at last, with the full realization of man's isolation from nature, the perspective is reduced so far that the pebbles may be seen as they should be, for human souls, ignorant armies. If nature is no warrant and no guide for man, then man is not acted upon, but acts. Confusion and ignorance must be faced, and life among men is clearly a battle. But all this is less important than it seems. For we toss *ourselves* to and fro. Our acts are our responsibility, not nature's. The road *is* ours, not the sea's.

As the power of nature has been progressively denigrated throughout the poem, we have assumed that man's power has been denigrated too. /138/ And so the narrator feels. But we know more than he does, for we judge his character, a thing he cannot do himself. And we finally see that, as nature's power reaches its nadir, only a sudden awareness of man's independent power can explain the pebbles' roar and make sense of the world we live in. The very fact that the narrator can make this image proves his control, for he is accepting the world as it is, transcending finally the last of many illusions in which man's power was denied. He has moved from his falsely peaceful window to the sea's edge, and finding no sea at all, has become fully human in his acceptance of the responsibility implied by the darkling plain. There is warrant for neither "joy, nor love, nor light" in nature, but still "we are here." And to stand with his love among the ignorant armies is to face his condition without recourse to misleading nature. His action proves that warrant for love comes from within, not from without, and that truth to each other is a matter of will, not fate. The narrator's action proves him better than the world he describes (the thought of the poem) should allow him to be, and so the gap between heroic action and despairing thought is the tragic theme. Initiative has been regained from nature which deluded or threatened, and since the narrator's first goal was understanding of his world and communion with his love (as Oedipus' aim was the pride of purging Thebes), he is a success, though not the kind of success he could have foreseen or wanted.

"Dover Beach" provides us cheer through the creation of a narrator whose gloomy thought is true, but whose action is so honest and so strong that it creates for us a perfect image of human worth. And it is thus like "Maud" in the toughmindedness of its theme as well as in its genre. The narrators of both poems attempt immersion in illusory certitudes—Maud's lover in his parents, in love, in empathy with a shell; Arnold's narrator in the sea, the moon-blanched land, the continuities of history and religion. But both narrators reject illusory certitudes for gratuitous acts which make them human; they immerse themselves at last in humanity, which is brutal and feverish but which is all that we can be sure of. With no illusions left, both narrators make action virtue. And there is little more that we can ask of tragedy.

A. Dwight Culler

Dover Beach*

Almost everything that we have been saying is drawn together and summarized in *Dover Beach*. The poem opens with a scene of pure natural loveliness: the sea calm, the tide full, the moon lying fair upon the straits. There is no sign of man except a single light which gleams for a moment and then is gone, and the great, reassuring cliffs of England stand, glimmering and vast, out in the tranquil bay. But, as Shakespeare tells us in *King Lear*,[1] "The murmuring surge / That on th'unnumber'd idle pebble chafes / Cannot be heard so high," and so, as the poet descends in imagination into the scene and exchanges the flat visual sense for the more penetrating auditory, he becomes aware of an element of discord of which he had not been conscious before. The sea is not calm, there is a "long line of spray"; the moon does not lie fair upon the straits, it "blanches" the land with a ghostly pallor; and the bay is not tranquil, for if you listen, you hear

the grating roar

Of pebbles which the waves draw back, and fling,
At their return, up the high strand,
Begin, and cease, and then again begin,
With tremulous cadence slow, and bring
The eternal note of sadness in.

---

* Reprinted from *Imaginative Reason*. New Haven: Yale University Press, 1966, pp. 39—41, by permission of the publisher and the author.

[1] IV.6.21–23. Arnold was well aware that the Dover cliffs are known as "Shakespeare's cliffs" because of their association with *King Lear*. (Letter to his mother, August 4, 1859, University of Virginia collection.) "Darkling," of course, is used in *King Lear*, I.4.237.

Wordsworth, writing from the opposite shore at Calais, had also declared, "It is a beauteous evening, calm and free;" and he also had turned from sight to sound and called to the child who was with him, "Listen!" But what he heard was— /40/

> the mighty Being is awake,
> And doth with his eternal motion make
> A sound like thunder—everlastingly.

Not so for Arnold. He moves the reader, not from natural beauty to transcendent Being, but from the illusion of natural beauty to the tragic fact of human experience.

In the second part of the poem the movement is repeated, but this time in terms, not of the natural scene, but of human history. For though the sea speaks eternally of sadness, it speaks to various people in various ways. To Sophocles in the classical age it spoke in a humanistic sense, of the turbid ebb and flow of a purely human misery. But to Arnold in the waning of the Christian age it speaks in a religious sense, of the slow withdrawal of the Sea of Faith. With mention of this Sea the poem retreats for a moment and recreates for the reader the sense of joyous fullness with which it first began. For in a lovely, feminine, protective image the Sea "round earth's shore / Lay like the folds of a bright girdle furl'd," following the ancient cosmology of Ocean Stream. But now, following the new cosmology of an open, exposed, precarious universe, it retreats "to the breath / Of the nightwind, down the vast edges drear / And naked shingles of the world." Readers have sometimes complained that the imagery of the poem is not unified, that we have no sea in the last section and no darkling plain in the first. But the naked shingles *are* the darkling plain, and that we have no sea in the last section is the very point of the poem. The sea has retreated from the world and left us "inland far," but unable, as in Wordsworth's poem, to

> see the Children sport upon the shore,
> And hear the mighty waters rolling evermore.

By two routes, then, through nature and through history, the poem has brought us to the reality of the darkling plain. For this is where the reader is finally placed, not in any religion of nature, which is an illusion, or of Chistianity, which is gone—not, in- /41/ deed, in any world which "seems" to lie before us like a "land of dreams," but here in this harsh, bitter actuality of our imaginative present. The image of the ignorant armies is drawn from Thucydides' famous account of the night-battle of Epipolae, a scene which Dr. Arnold apparently made a commonplace among his pupils as a symbol of the intellectual confusion of the modern age. But whether we imagine ourselves with Thucydides on the heights of Epipolae, or with Gloucester on the cliffs of Dover, or with Oedipus at Colonnus, all can say, "We are here as on a darkling plain." That is the true image to describe the human condition.

One would not go far wrong, then, if he took from this most famous of Arnold's poems its most famous phrase and said that this is the central statement which Arnold makes about the human condition: "We are here as on a darkling plain." No Romantic poet ever made such a statement, and no other Victorian prior to Hardy made it with such uncompromising severity. It is only the modern poet who has followed Arnold in his vision of the tragic and alienated condition of man. In this sense, Arnold may be called a modern poet, and it is certain that he would have accepted the designation. He considered that his poems, more than those of his contemporaries, represented "the main movement of mind of the last quarter of a century." "It might be fairly urged," he wrote to his mother, "that I have less poetical sentiment than Tennyson, and less intellectual vigour and abundance than Browning; yet, because I have perhaps more of a fusion of the two than either of them, and have more regularly applied that fusion to the main line of modern development, I am likely enough to have my turn, as they have had theirs."[2]

---

[2] *Letters of Matthew Arnold, 1848–1888*, ed. G. W. E. Russell (New York, London, 1895), II, 10.

Gale H. Carrithers, Jr.

Missing Persons
on Dover Beach?*

Is it illusion? All readers love "Dover Beach," but all feel defensive?
Scholarly critiques and class discussions alike tend to conclude either
with a dying fall or a stamping foot. Is there, alas, something wrong
with the poem?

The poem brilliantly fuses narrative and drama, and the traditional
modes of reflection and celebration. No fault there. It celebrates the
moment of reflection by dramatizing it as a thing of poignant riches.
Such a moment comes to look very much like that "certain margin
of tranquillity" without which (as Ortega y Gasset reminds us) "truth
succumbs."[1]

Nor is inadvertence or local disjunction the trouble. True, the Tinker
and Lowry handbook not only offers helpful glosses, but also provides evidence that the poem was conceived and drafted in the 1850's.
The idea for the last stanza may go back even to the year of Arnold's
honeymoon, 1851, or earlier, for all we know. But in any case, the
poem aptly unites reflection with a dramatic situation. Even as the
speaker takes note of benighted France and majestic, enlightened
England, he savors something which will be (presumably) more
gratifying to his beloved, the sweet night air, and calls her to the
window and the view. Tinker and Lowry point out that *sweet* was
substituted for *hush'd*. Seemingly the change yields not only dramatic gain, but clearer thematic contrast with the somewhat ill wind of
lines 26 and 27. This was only one of several revisions Arnold made

---

* Reprinted from *Modern Language Quarterly*, XXVI (June, 1965), 264–66, by
permission of the journal and the author.
[1] José Ortega y Gasset, "The Self and the Other" (1939), trans. Willard R. Trask
in *The Dehumanization of Art and Other Writings on Art and Culture* (Garden
City, N.Y., 1956), p. 186.

between manuscript and /265/ final version. The drama does not interrupt the meditation: that continues quickly with a typically Arnoldian reservation, "Only . . . you hear the grating roar," which animates the remaining eight lines of the stanza. The observant speaker's imagination is at work, apprehending those structural kinships which are the essence of symbol, as he and his beloved regard this scene "blanch'd," silvered, distanced by the moon, that standard Romantic and Arnoldian image for the imagination. He recognizes the sensory kinship of Greek and English poet confronted with natural vehicles for metaphor, and he gradually makes the complex transition from majestic, enlightened England to *"high* strand" (revised from *steep,* and from *barr'd*), to "find . . . in the sound a thought" of England high and dry, equally distant from Aegean Sea and Sophocles' town, Galilee and Christ's town. "Bright girdle," incidentally, insists more strongly than the manuscript "bright garment" that the sea of water and faith alike never in human memory covered all, and it hints of the vivid sash a Near Eastern figure could be supposed to wear. A nineteenth-century English gentleman might wear a bright garment, but probably not a "bright girdle."

Greek and Hebraic visions of reality are alike unavailable to the speaker, because they are either (1) too remote, or (2) too imperfect or corrupt. If 1, and there is no viable third formulation of reality, then the poem sags into a case history of neurotic apathy or egotism. The poem is oriented away from this flatness, but with ambiguous success. The poem gestures in the direction of 2, but the misery and the faithlessness scarcely become concrete and real in the poem, being merely asserted and only indirectly manifested in the lover's malaise. On the other hand, when the speaker says *"we* find also in the sound a thought," his imaginative remark implies faith in his beloved's sympathy. He continues his act of secular faith, turning from the window to her, from the seeming-world "before us like a land of dreams," thereby apparently reaffirming their sympathy and somewhat languid happiness in one another. Whether his judgment of the world is absolutely true or not, or is even realized within the poem, it is a consequential evaluation available to sane men, to one's friend or enemy or one's self, a judgment well within the precincts of poetry. The couple, then, do not live and move and have their being in the sea of faith, nor even on the beach, but on the adjacent darkling plain, and they make their obeisance "to one another," so their love must bear a considerable structural and thematic weight: it is the vehicle to carry such residues as /266/ accrue to the couple from classical and Christian past, the hinted-at proportional patterns of pity, faithfulness, rationality, order, perhaps love itself, localized to the couple's measure. And that love must, among the reciprocal contributions of the poem's parts, be the major force validating the speaker as a man, as a humanely capable enunciator of the judgments he pronounces, a person not simply a mouth biting empty air. The poem demands, in short, a stylistic rendering of the love sufficiently dynamic to show that the couple have not localized their proportional patterns of value to the vanishing point.

Arnold has invoked a large historical and geographical picture, and with it considerable intellectual and imaginative intensity. But in this poem about a man and his beloved contemplating these matters, the inclusive passion does not sufficiently appear, either directly or by definitive contrast, even though we may like to *assume* that the passion is somewhere or somehow there.[2] Are we then given two non-persons embracing nullity amid splendors of scene and history? Neuroses, we knew, are matters of degree, and let him who is without any cast the first stone. Some tensions dramatized in the poem are aesthetically fruitful exactly because of such universality. Are they warm people or cold people? Are they confused people or sure people? Are they committed people or hesitant and diffident poeple? Are they people who momentarily desire this little room to be an everywhere (whether or not that is possible)? But the uncertainty, built in and unresolvable as to whether the people matter (as people we know matter) or lack the life-in-value and consequentiality to matter or to make even temporarily the commitment the speaker urges, or a commitment to the darkling plain, *that* uncertainty weakens the poem. Just there, rather than in a switch from ebb and flow on moonlit watery plain to ebb and flow on dark and earthy plain, would seem to be the place at which the considerable resonances —literal, conscious, subconscious—of ocean, moon, dream, historical vista, and the night are not rounded off.

---

[2] For a view which I take to agree roughly with part of this, see the hilarious spoof by Anthony Hecht, "The Dover Bitch, a Criticism of Life," *Transatlantic Review*, No. 1 (1960) pp. 57–58. For partially contrasting recent views, see, for example, Rodney Delesanta "Arnold's 'Dover Beach,'" *Explicator*, XVIII (1959), Item 7; W. Stacy Johnson, *The Voices of Matthew Arnold* (New Haven, 1961), pp. 90–94, 117, 136; U. C. Knoepflmacher, "Dover Revisited: The Wordsworthian Matrix," *Victorian Poetry*, I (1963), 17–26.

Norman N. Holland

Psychological Depths
and "Dover Beach"*

Psychoanalysis and literary analysis have mingled uneasily ever since 15 October 1897, when Freud simultaneously found in himself and in Hamlet "love of the mother and jealousy of the father." Psychoanalysis, it turned out, could say many interesting things about plays and novels. Unfortunately, it did not do at all well with the analysis of poems. In the symbolistic psychoanalysis of 1915 or so, poems became simply assemblages of the masculine or feminine symbols into which psychoanalysis seemed then to divide the world. Poems, often, were reduced to mere dreams—for old-style psychoanalysis could look only at the content, not the form, of poetry.

Literary critics may fare better with new-style psychoanalysis—indeed, not so new, for one could date it from Anna Freud's *The Ego and the Mechanisms of Defense* in 1936. This later phase of psychoanalysis takes into account defenses or defense mechanisms—that is, ways of dealing with drives or impulses so as to ward off anxiety and to adapt drives to reality in a positive or useful way. A literary critic recognizes this concept of defense as something very like what Kenneth Burke would call a "strategy" or "trope." A psychology that can deal with defenses can deal with poems in terms of form as well as of content, for form is to content in literature as, in life, defense is to impulse. I would also like to suggest that because today's psychoanalysis can look at both literary form and literary content, we can from literary works frame a hypothesis as to the fundamental psychological patterns of drive and defense in a given culture. Such a psychological pattern should in turn tell us why some literary forms succeed in a given culture and others fail.

* Reprinted from *Victorian Studies*, IX (Supplement, September, 1965), 5–28, by permission of the journal and the author.

My test case is Victorian England. I would like to see, first, what an understanding of defenses can add to the conventional explication of a poem. Second, I would like to see what a knowledge of defenses can tell us for literary history—specifically, the literary history of Victorian England. Naturally, then, we should look at a Victorian poem, perhaps *the* Victorian poem. /6/

"Dover Beach" (according to *The Case for Poetry*) is the most widely reprinted poem in the language. Certainly, it seems like the most widely explicated, once you begin researching it. Let me try to summarize in a few paragraphs what a dozen or so of the most useful explicators and annotators have to say.[1]

First, the date. Arnold wrote a draft of the first three stanzas on notes for *Empedocles on Etna*. He had completed the poem, then, in the summer of 1850 (Tinker) or 1851 (Baum). Depending on which summer you settle for, the poem refers to some rendezvous with Marguerite or to Arnold's seaside honeymoon with Frances.

The reference to Sophocles in the second stanza is somewhat vague, but it seems clear that for the final image Arnold had in mind the episode in Book VII of Thucydides where, during the ill-fated Sicilian expedition, the Athenian troops became confused during the night battle at Epipolae. The enemy learned their password, and the Athenians went down to disastrous defeat (Tinker).

The poem itself moves from light to darkness, paralleling its thematic movement as a whole from faith to disillusionment (*Case for*

---

[1] Since explications necessarily overlap, it is hard to give credit where credit is due, but I will try. To avoid a cumbersome series of footnotes, I will simply give in parentheses after a given statement, what seems to me the most appropriate name or title, referring to the following list of explications: Paull F. Baum, *Ten Studies in the Poetry of Matthew Arnold* (Durham, N. C., 1958), pp. 85–97. Louis Bonnerot, *Matthew Arnold, Poéte: Essai de biographie psychologique* (Paris, 1947), p. 203. *The Case for Poetry*, eds. Frederick L. Gwynn, Ralph W. Condee, and Arthur O. Lewis, Jr. (Englewood Cliffs, 1954), pp. 17, 19, and "Teacher's Manual," pp. 14–15. Rodney Delasanta, *The Explicator*, XVIII (1959), 7. Elizabeth Drew, *Poetry: A Modern Guide to its Understanding and Enjoyment* (New York, 1959), pp. 221–223. Gerhard Friedrich, "A Teaching Approach to Poetry," *English Journal*, XLIX (1960), 75–81. Frederick L. Gwynn, *Explicator*, VIII (1960), 46. Wendell Stacy Johnson, "Matthew Arnold's Dialogue," *University of Kansas City Review*, XXVII (1960), 109–116. Wendell Stacy Johnson, *The Voices of Matthew Arnold: An Essay in Criticism* (New Haven, 1961), pp. 90–94. J. D. Jump, *Matthew Arnold* (London, 1955), pp. 67–68 and 81. J. P. Kirby, *Explicator*, I (1943), 42. Murray Krieger, " 'Dover Beach' and the Tragic Sense of Eternal Recurrence," *University of Kansas City Review*, XXIII (1956), 73–79. Gene Montague, "Arnold's 'Dover Beach' and 'The Scholar Gypsy,' " *Explicator*, XVIII (1959), 15. Frederick A. Pottle, *Explicator*, II (1944), 45. Norman C. Stageberg, *Explicator*, IX (1951), 34. C. B. Tinker and H. F. Lowry, *The Poetry of Matthew Arnold: A Commentary* (London, 1940), pp. 173–178. I do not know of any psychoanalytic explications except that referred to in no. 7.

Poetry), or from the wholly literal to the wholly metaphorical, from small abstractions to large ones, from past to present (Johnson, 1961). At the same time, the poem builds on a series of dualisms or contrasts. The most ironic of them is the contrast between the tranquil scene and the restless incertitude of the speaker (Kirby), but the most powerful is that between the land and the sea. The sea, in particular, evokes a rich variety of symbolic values: a sense of time and constant change, of vitality—the waters of baptism and birth—also a sense of blankness, /7/ formlessness, and mystery (Johnson, 1961). One could think of the land-sea conflict as one between man and nature or present and past (Krieger) or between the dry, critical mind (note the pun) and a natural, spontaneous, self-sufficient existence represented by the sea (Johnson, 1960). One could even think of the sea as a kind of Providence failing to master the Necessity represented by the eternal note of the pebbles (Delasanta). The sea is stable, as faith is; yet it has its ebb and flow and spray, turbid like human misery. Similarly, the land is itself solid and coherent, but its pebbles and shingles are atomistic and agitated (Gwynn), as though the point of misery and conflict were right at the edge or mingling of land and sea (*Case for Poetry*).

The dualism of the poem shows in its structure as well. Each of the four stanzas divides quite markedly into two parts. In stanzas one, three, and four, the first part is hopeful; the second undercuts illusion with reality (Krieger). In exehy case, illusion is presented in terms of sight, and reality in terms of sound (Delasanta). Thus, the poem moves back and forth from optimistic images of sight to pessimistic images of sound. We can perhaps think of hearing as "the more contiguous sense," the "more subtle sense" (Krieger), but the sounds that dominate the poem are alarms of battle and grating and withdrawing roars (Gwynn).

The poem builds on this manifold dualism, but at the same time it presses steadily forward, with each stanza referring to the one preceding (Krieger). There is a kind of five-part structure as the poem moves from a setting to a dramatic situation to a transitional passage (the second stanza) to an ethical, philosophical comment (the third stanza); finally, that philosophical comment converts to a seemingly unrelated image with a shock of abruptness and strangeness (Montague).

The first stanza gives us a scene so richly laden in values as to make us feel a kind of total satisfaction or utter completeness. Then, at the word "only" the scene lapses into the harsh sound and message of the pebbles (Krieger). Yet even in the first line, the word "to-night" hints at the transitory quality of this fullness and satisfaction (Friedrich), as do in the third and fourth lines the appearance and disappearance of the light from the French coast. The French lights, though, contrast with the stable cliffs of England which "stand,/Glimmering and vast" and so balance the French ebb and flow with permanency. The magnificent "Begin, and cease, and then again begin" also acts out in its rhythm the inexorable quality of the struggle (Krieger). The first stanza closes with the musical words "cadence" and "note," a humanistic overtone which bridges to Sophocles (Gwynn). But the first stanza also ends /8/ with the "grating roar," a harsh sound that shatters the calm of the opening and sends the poet more drastically off to the Ægæan (Drew).

The shift from the first stanza to the second represents a shift from the here and now to the everywhere and always (Krieger) ; the eternal note of sadness and the battle between sea and land merge past and present, we and they. The third stanza returns to the sea as complete and self-sufficient, then breaks at the "but" into a disillusionment expressed as sound (Krieger). The light fades as faith did (Stageberg) and leads us into the last half of the stanza whose falling rhythm and open vowels pour us relentlessly over into the final stanza (Jump).

That last stanza states the theme explicitly for the first time (Kirby), the contrast between seeming perfection and real chaos (Krieger), between the world as an illusion of beauty (Pottle) and the harsh reality of life (Drew). The last three lines give us a startlingly new image (Baum), harsh and surprising (Jump), one wholly metaphorical as against the otherwise wholly realistic setting of the poem (Johnson, 1961). Once we get over the shock of the image, though, we can see that it is not discontinuous, but progresses logically from what has gone before: the "darkling plain" continues the earlier contrast between the land and the sea (Kirby) and extends and enlarges the earlier image of the "naked shingles" (Kirby, Drew). The rhyme-word "light" halfway in the stanza and the subsequent "flight" and "night" take us back to the opening rhymes "to-night" and "light" (Kirby), giving us a sense of closure and completeness. Similarly, the first three stanzas mixed lines of five feet and less and used rhymes in an unpredictable way, though one that gave us a vague sense of recurrence. The last stanza, though, is rigorously rhymed *abba cddcc* with the break at the break in thought; and only the opening and closing lines have irregular lengths—the body of the stanza consists of seven five-foot lines (Krieger). Even so, within this heavy regularity, consonants clash to fill out in sound the sense of the final batle image (Drew).

The poem ends, thus, as it began, in duality. A sense of twoness runs through the various attempts by the explicators to state the idea that informs and pervades the poem: "the poet's melancholy awareness of the terrible incompatibility between illusion and reality" (Delasanta); "the repetitive inclusiveness of the human condition and its purposeless gyrations," "the tragic sense of eternal recurrence" (Krieger); "the sea-rhythm of the world in general and also of the poet's soul which finds itself mysteriously in accord with that cosmic pulse" (Bonnerot).

In general, the poem moves back and forth between here and there, past and present, land and sea, love and battle, but more impor-
/9/ tantly between sweet sight and disillusioning sound, between appearance and reality. What informs the poem, then, is an attempt to re-create in a personal relationship the sweet sight of stability and permanence which the harsh sound of the actual ebb and flow of reality negates.

Now, with all these explicatory riches, what can psychoanalysis add to a reading of the poem? Like all explications, these treat the poem as an objective fact, which it is—in part. The part we prize, though, is our subjective experience of the poem, the interaction of the poem with what we bring to the poem—our own habits of mind, character, past experience, and present feelings that act with the poem "out there" to make a total experience "in here." Psychoanalysis is that science that tries to speak objectively about subjective states; and, by the same token, the psychoanalytic critic tries to talk objectively about his subjective experience of the poem.

To me, "Dover Beach" is a tremendously peaceful and gently melancholy poem. And that is somewhat surprising, since, after all, it is a poem at least partly about disillusionment, loss of faith, despair—why should such a poem seem peaceful or satisfying? In effect I am asking the same question Aristotle (and indeed, Arnold himself) asked about tragedy: how is it that the most painful experiences can be felt as pleasurable in works of art?[2] A psychoanalyst would answer:

---

2 "Though the objects themselves may be painful to see," notes Aristotle, "we delight to view the most realistic representations of them in art. . . . The explanation is to be found in a further fact: to be learning something is the greatest of pleasures not only to the philosopher but also to the rest of mankind, however small their capacity for it: the reason of the delight is that one is at the same time learning—gathering the meaning of things." And Arnold: "In presence of the most tragic circumstances, represented in a work of Art, the feeling of enjoyment, as is well known, may still subsist: the representation of the most utter calamity, of the liveliest anguish is not sufficient to destroy it. . . . What . . . are the

"Because art imitates life." That is, we approach life through a series of interacting impulses and defenses, and a work of art offers us a ready-made interaction of impulses and defenses. When we take in Arnold's poem, /10/ experience it, we take in the drives the poem expresses. We also take in the poem's way of dealing with those drives, satisfying them and giving pleasure. And, further, the work of art typically transmutes patterns of impulse and defense into moral and intellectual meaning, a wholeness and completeness that our impulses and defenses do not have in everyday life.

Let us, then, talk about "Dover Beach" as a subjective experience. The poem gives me a tremendous feeling of pacification, tranquility, soothing peace.[3] Why? Because, I think, the poem offers such a heavy, massive set of defenses. We begin with the exquisite description of the seascape in which everything is vast, tranquil, calm—any disturbance in that calmness, such as the word "to-night" in the first line, the appearance and disappearance of the light from France, is immediately balanced and corrected. Only after this strong reassurance does Arnold give us a stronger disturbance, the eternal note of sadness—and, immediately, he flees in space and time to Sophocles and the Ægæan; he turns the disturbing thought into literature—and far-off, ancient literature at that. And thus defended, he can permit the disturbance to come back again: "we/Find also in the sound a thought," but even as he returns to the here and now, he defends again. He turns the feeling of disturbance into an intellectual, sym-

---

situations, from the representation of which, though accurate, no poetical enjoyment can be derived? They are those in which the suffering finds no vent in action; in which a continuous state of mental distress is prolonged, unrelieved by incident, hope, or resistance; in which there is everything to be endured, nothing to be done. In such situations there is inevitably something morbid, in the description of them something monotonous" (Preface to *Poems*, 1853).

Neither Aristotle nor Arnold had a psychology adequate to the problem, but the insights of both are sound, as far as they go. Translated into modern terms, they are saying that painful events can give pleasure in tragedy because the work of art provides defensive ways of escaping the pain and turning it into meaningful pleasure. Aristotle, typically Greek, stresses intellectualization as a defense. Arnold, typically Victorian, stresses action. I, typically twentieth-century, would say you have to analyze the defenses and adaptations of particular tragedies, tragedy by tragedy, before generalizing.

[3] I realize that others find in the poem, not this sense of peace, but an ultimate feeling of failure and despair as, for example, in the explications of Delasanta and Krieger (though Bonnerot finds the pacification). Even so, if I can discover by analyzing my own reaction the drives the poem stirs up in me and the defenses the poem presents for dealing with those drives, then I can understand the different reactions of others for whom those defenses are less congenial or adequate.

bolic, metaphorical statement, in a line that never fails to jar me by its severely schematic and allegorical quality: "The Sea of Faith." Defended again, he can again return to the disturbing sound, and in the most pathetic lines of the poem he lets it roll off the edge of the earth in long, slow vowels. In the last stanza, he brings in the major defense of the poem, "Ah, love, let us be true/To one another." He offers us as a defense a retreat into a personal relationship of constancy with another person; and so defended, he can give us the final, terrible image of the ignorant armies that clash by night. In short, the poem gives me—and others, too—this tremendous feeling of tranquillity because I am over-protected; because Arnold has offered me strong defenses against the disturbance the poem deals with—even before he reveals the disturbance itself in the final lines.

Further, that disturbance itself is never very clearly presented. It is described obliquely, by negatives. For example, the sea is calm "tonight"—and the "to-night" acts as a qualification: there are other nights /11/ when the sea is not calm, but we do not see them. The window in line six comes as something of a surprise—it is as though the poet were reaching back for his companion even as he reaches out to take in the seascape, a special form of the dualism that pervades the poem. But the disturbance is dim and oblique. We do not see the room or the person addressed, only the window facing away from them. The "grating roar" of the pebbles is humanized and softened into music: "cadence" and "note." "The turbid ebb and flow of human misery" seems metaphorized, distanced, more than a little vague. The world, we are told, seems like but is not a land of dreams, but what it is we are not told. We are told that faith is gone; and, while most critics seem to assume Arnold's "Faith" means religious faith, that, it seems to me, is only one of its meanings. The word "Faith" is not explained until the last stanza and is then only explained by what is missing: the ability to clothe the world with joy and love and light, to find in the world certitude, peace, and help for pain. But the poem does not tell us what the world is like without these things, except, metaphorically, in the image of the ignorant armies. In other words, the poem offers us not only massive defenses, but also a specific line of defense: we do not see the disturbance itself; we only see what it is not.

There is a second specific line of defense. This poem sees and hears intensely; it gives us pleasure through what we see and hear, but at the same time the seeing and hearing operate defensively. Often, in life, to see and hear one thing intensely may serve to avoid seeing and hearing something else.[4] In this poem, we look at and listen to the sea, the shingle, to Sophocles—what are we not looking at? What is being hidden from us that we are curious about, that we would like to see? I trust you will not think me irreverent if I remind you that this a poem /12/ at least partly about a pair of lovers together at night. I cannot speak for everyone, but as for myself, I am curious as to what they are up to. The poem, however, tells me very little, for only six of its thirty-seven lines deal directly with the girl; and three of those six are so general they could refer to all mankind.

This is another case in which the poem shows us something indirectly, defensively, by showing us what it is not. The poet treats the particular here-and-now relationship between himself and the girl as the always-and-everywhere condition of all mankind. He defines the girl as a substitute for the world: let us be true to one another for the world proved false. He defines his wished-for relationship with the girl indirectly, obliquely, negatively, by stating what his relationship with the world at large is not.

What, then, is this world which the girl must replace? As the explicators point out, it is a world rather sharply divided into two aspects roughly corresponding to illusion and reality or, in the terms of the poem itself, the sight of a bright, calm seascape representing a world with faith, and the sound of agitated pebbles, one without faith.

The theme of sound reminds us of the importance of the sounds of the poem itself, and particularly the rhyme and rhythm so beau-

---

[4] Arnold's own psyche is no part of the present paper. It is interesting, though, to note how often the theme of seeing or being seen occurs in Arnold's writings. He praises, for exmple, one "Who saw life steadily and saw it whole" ("To a Friend"). He spoke through Empedocles of "Gods we cannot see," and in "Self-Deception" of a parental "Power beyond our seeing." As suggested in the text, Arnold often looked intensely at one thing as a way of not seeing something else.

At the same time, though, this kind of intense seeing and hearing can operate defensively in another way. To say I am seeing can be a way of saying I am not being seen, and in Arnold's poetry the motif of not being seen or heard crops out repeatedly. Callicles, for example, must not be seen by Empedocles as the philosopher is about to jump into the burning crater. Neither Sohrab nor Merope recognizes (i.e., sees) his son. One can fairly guess, I think, at the poet's escaping the eyes of his parents, "He, who sees us through and through" ("A Farewell"), or a Mother Nature watching her struggling child ("Morality"). "I praise," he writes, "the life which slips away / Out of the light and mutely" ("Early Death and Fame"), such as the scholar-gypsy or Obermann. Thus, in "Dover Beach," Arnold treats the world, not as seeing himself and his love, but as indifferent, not caring, not offering help for pain: as "*ignorant* armies." One is reminded of the children in "Stanzas from the Grand Chartreuse," "secret from the eyes of all," watching distant soldiers march to war.

tifully worked into the sense at three points: line twelve, "Begin, and cease, and then again begin"; the long withdrawal of the last four lines of stanza three; finally, the clotted consonants that accompany the image of the ignorant armies. It is worth noting that these points where the sound becomes particularly strong are all points of disillusionment in the poem. In general, strong rhyme seems linked in the poem to passages of expectation or trust or acceptance; strong rhythm seems linked to a sense of reality and solidity. Thus, the rhymes are strong in stanza two, the intellectual acceptance of disillusionment, and in stanza four, the emotional acceptance. Rhythm is strong at the opening of the poem with its great feeling of regularity, solidity, thereness.

In the first three stanzas of this poem of division and dualism, rhyme and rhythm tend to be divorced from each other. At points where we are strongly aware of the rhythm, the rhyme tends to disappear from consciousness or even from the poem. Conversely, at points of very regular rhyme, as in stanza two, the rhythm becomes irregular and tends to disintegrate. This sound pattern seems to be a part of the general defensive strategy of the poem—to divide the world and deal with it in parts, to show us things by showing us what they are not. Similarly, Arnold divides each of the lines from two to six halfway—and this, again, is part of the general strategy of division in the poem, but also, /13/ as all through the poem, a way of dealing with the world of the poem as he deals with the world described by the poem: dividing it in two to deal with it in parts. Finally, at the close of the poem, not only rhythm, but also rhyme becomes strong; there is a strengthening of defensive form as the poem comes to its moment of greatest stress and distress in content. Rhyme, rhythm, and sense all come together at the close to make us experience in ourselves the poem's final rhymed acceptance of a disturbing reality expressed as rhythmic sound.

Rhythmic sound itself seems to be the disillusioning influence which the poem struggles to accept. Obviously, we need to ask what the emotional significance of that rhythm is. Consider, for a moment, the two senses, sight and hearing. Why do we speak of "feasting" one's eyes or "devouring" with a look? Why do we speak of "the voice" of conscience or of God as "the word"?

"Dover Beach" taps our earliest experience of our two major senses. Sight, the child comes to first. As early as the third month of life, a baby can recognize a human face as such. By the fourth or fifth month, he can distinguish the face of the person who feeds and fondles him from other faces. Sight becomes linked in our minds to being fed, to a nurturing mother. Thus, for example, in "Dover Beach," the strong sight images of the first five lines lead into a demand that a woman come, a taste image ("sweet"), and even, if we identify kinaesthetically with the poet, an inhaling of that sweet night air. In infancy, sight becomes associated with a taking in, specifically a taking in from a mother in whom we have faith, whom we expect to give us joy, love, light, certitude, peace, help for pain. Our first disillusionment in life comes as that nurturing figure fails to stand calm, full, fair, vast, tranquil, always there, but instead retreats, withdraws, ebbs and flows. And the poem makes us hear this withdrawal.

Our important experience with hearing comes later than seeing. Not until we begin to understand words does hearing begin to convey as much to us as sight does, and it seems to be in the nature of things that a good deal of what the one or two year old child hears is— "Don't." We experience sound as a distancing from a parent, often a corrective, not something we anticipate and expect, but something we must willy-nilly put up with, since we cannot shut our ears as we can our eyes. In "Dover Beach," then, what the poet wishes for from the world, but knows will not come, is the kind of fidelity, "Faith," or gratification a child associates with the sight of his mother, but the sound the poet hears routs his expectations. And the poem, by associating sight with the world as we wish and hope it would be, and sound as a corrector of /14/ that wish, finds in us a responsive note, for this has been part of our experience, too.

But what, specifically, does the harsh sound of grating pebbles bring to our minds, particularly as Arnold describes it in the poem? For one thing, as the explicators show, the point of misery and conflict seems to come right at the joining or mingling of land and sea. For another, the disturbance seems to lie in its very periodicity, its rhythm. Where the opening seascape is very solidly there, calm, full, tranquil—"the cliffs of England *stand*" (and the internal rhyme demands heavy stress)—the disturbance is an ebb and flow, a withdrawing, a retreat, a being drawn back and flung up; the waves "Begin, and cease, and then again begin." And slowly, what was simply a harsh, rhythmical sound gains other overtones. The "bright girdle" is withdrawn and we are left with "naked shingles." The world does not "lie before us like a land of dreams." Rather, the "Begin, and cease, and then again begin" has become a naked clash by night. There is a well-nigh universal sexual symbolism in this heard-but-not-seen naked fighting by night. The poem is evoking in me, at least, and perhaps in many readers, primitive feelings about "things that go bump in the night"—disturbing, frightening, but exciting at the same time, like a horror movie. This is one way Arnold's poem turns our experience of disillusionment or despair into a satisfying one, namely, through the covert gratification we get from this final image. A psychoanalyst would recognize a "primal scene fantasy." Arnold is talking about hearing a sexual "clash by night," just as children fantasy sex as fight.[5] At the same time, the image operates defensively as well. This poem tells about a pair of lovers in a sexual situation; as elsewhere in the poem, the image deflects our attention from that sexual situation and sublimates it into a distant, literary, and moral experience, a darkling plain from Thucydides.

The conventional explicators have found some logic underlying that final startling image: a logical development from brightness to darkness, from the pebble beach to the darkling plain. Ordinary explication, however, offers little basis for the armies, while psychological explication offers considerable. The poem begins with a world which is very solidly there, a world which is seen, a world which is invested with a faith like a child's trust in the sight of his nurturing mother. The poem moves into sound, to the later, harsher sense, and with it to the sounds of withdrawal and retreat. Thus, the sound of the ocean shifts from the /15/ rhythm of waves to the more permanent, even geological withdrawal of the "Sea of Faith." The feeling is one of permanent decay, a sense of harsh reality akin to a child's growing knowledge that his mother does not exist for him alone, that she has a life of her own and wishes of her own which cause her to go away from him and come back, to retreat and withdraw. The final image brings in a still stronger feeling of rhythmic withdrawal, a feeling like that of a child's excited but frightened vague awareness of the naked, nighttime rhythmic sound of that other, separate adult life. It does not lie there like a land of dreams—rather, it is violent and brutal; the bright girdle is withdrawn and bodies clash by night. Roughly, we could say that the lovely appearances seen in the poem—the moonlight, the cliffs of England, the stillness—correspond to a faith in a mother. The harsh sounds of withdrawal heard in the poem correspond to the disillusioning knowledge of one's mother's relationship with father, the latter expressed perhaps as Sophocles or Thucydides (Arnold's father did edit Thucydides). In the manner

---

[5] In the discussion following the reading of this paper, it was suggested to me that the sexual symbolism is even more exact than stated in the text. The "darkling plain" may suggest to us, unconsciously, the nuptial bed, the "struggle" a man's activity and the "flight" a woman's passivity in the sexual situation.

of a dream, the two individuals hidden in the poem, a father and mother, are disguised as two multitudes, two "armies"; and they, usually all-seeing, all-wise, become in the violent moment of passion, "ignorant."

But we still have not answered the question, How does the poem turn this disturbing awareness of withdrawal into a pleasurable experience? So far, we have talked only about the defenses the poem uses: the flight to Sophocles, symbolic disguise, intellectualization, most important, division, keeping a sharp difference between the seen appearance and the heard reality. But such defenses can only prevent unpleasure—how can the poem give up pleasure and create a rounded experience?

The pleasure lies in that aspect of the poem that the commentators almost without exception ignore (thus proving the strength and success of Arnold's defensive maneuvers). Let me remind you again that this is a poem that talks about a man and a women in love and alone together. Yet how oddly and how brilliantly the poem handles this problem of stationing its speaker! For the first five lines we have only the vaguest inkling of where he is: looking at a seascape near Dover. Then, in line six, we suddenly learn, first, that he is indoors, second, that there is someone with him, someone whom he wishes to take in what he is taking in. Yet the poem does nothing more with this sudden placing. Instead, the curiosity it arouses, the faint feeling of disturbance, is displaced onto the sound heard in the lines after line six—another way of making us feel the sound as disturbing, and as complicating the scene.

The next two stanzas do little more with the problem of stationing. Stanza two places the speaker in space—by showing us where he /16/ is not, the Ægæan; then, it places him by "a distant northern sea." The "we" of line eighteen has all the ambiguities of the editorial we —it could be the poet as a public speaker, the poet and his companion, or the poet and all his contemporaries. Stanza three places the poet in time, again, negatively: not "once" when the sea of faith was full, but "now"—again, something a bit vague and something we already know. Then, suddenly, line twenty-nine tells us something new again—that he is in love with his companion. Their relationship thus emerges from the rest of the poem like shadowy figures materializing,[6] until, at last, only two lines from the close, the poem

---

[6] This, too, is a recurring theme in Arnold's writing—a sense of the true state of affairs emerging like a human figure. Thus, the 1853 Preface to *Poems* speaks of a myth in the Greek spectator's mind "traced in its bare outlines . . . as a group of statuary, faintly seen, at the end of a long and dark vista: then came

firmly stations the poet and his love: "And we are here." Even here, though, there is some blurring, for the "we" could be the editorial we of stanza two as well as the we of you-and-I. And, further, we are no sooner "here" than we are there, metaphorically flown to the darkling plain swept by ignorant armies.

In short, the stationing of the poet and his love involves a good deal of shifting and ambiguity. As always in this poem, the poem is telling us what things are obliquely, by telling us what they are not. The ambiguity about where the poet and his love are suggests that we look to see where they are in another sense—and there, indeed, we can locate them quite precisely: they are right there in lines six, nine, eighteen, twenty-four, twenty-nine, and thirty-five. They occur precisely at the points of division in the poem where it moves from sight to sound, from appearance to reality, or, in stanza two, from a far-off, literary Sophocles to the here and now of "we" by the northern sea. To put it another way, the lovers come between the two kinds of experience the poem creates. This is the importance of the phrase, "And we are here," which makes us feel the closure and completeness of the poem. Read over the last lines with variant phrasings to see the importance of that clause:

> . . . nor peace, nor help for pain;
> And the world is, as on a darkling plain
> Swept with confused alarms of struggle and flight,
> Where ignorant armies clash by night. /17/
> . . . nor peace, nor help for pain;
> And I am here, as on a darkling plain
> Swept with confused alarms of struggle and flight,
> Where ignorant armies clash by night.

The poem needs the finality both of being *here* and of being *we*, for this is the poem's ultimate defense.

Stanza one opened with sight, taken as reassuring, constant, full, and closed with sound sensed as a kind of corruption penetrating the fair sight. Stanzas two and three fled this conflict both in time and space, and fled it in another way through the poet's universalizing of

---

the Poet, embodying outlines. . . . the light deepened upon the group; more and more it revealed itself to the riveted gaze of the spectator: until at last, when the final words were spoken, it stood before him in broad sunlight, a model of immortal beauty." Similarly, at the opening of the 1869 Preface to *Essays in Criticism*, he describes Truth as a "mysterious Goddess" who, even if approached obliquely, can only be seen in outline, while, "He who will do nothing but fight impetuously towards her . . . is inevitably destined to run his head into the folds of the black robe in which she is wrapped." I am reminded of Empedocles' rushing into the crater.

his feelings, spreading them over all time, all space, all peoples. And yet this defense leaves him disillusioned, and he turns at the opening of stanza four to the girl as a way of dealing with the problem.

He begins by saying, "Ah, love, let us be true/To one another"; and "true" is the key word. He wants to re-create in his relationship with her the lost sense of faith; he wants her to be "true," not to withdraw as the earlier sight had done. "True" also suggests that the relationship of the two, the poet and his love, will not be like the relationship of the two halves of the world as he sees them. The lovers will not corrupt or contradict one another as the two halves of the world do—rather, they will be "true/To one another."

The last stanza then moves into a series of lists that act out the poet's feeling toward the world that has failed him, that though it seems

> So various, so beautiful, so new,
> Hath really neither joy, nor love, nor light,
> Nor certitude, nor peace, nor help for pain.

The lists give us a feeling of inclusiveness, of taking it all in, but the lists are negative, "neither," "nor," "nor"—so that it is precisely the inclusiveness that is rejected; precisely the fact that the world negates all the things the poet wants to take in that leads to the rejection of the world. Here is the first half of the poem's strategy: to try to take in joy, love, light, certitude, peace, help for pain; but, upon finding some one part of the world that negates these things, to reject all the world. A psychoanalyst would speak here of denial: the poet must deny whatever conflicts with his wish to be given joy, love, light, and the rest. In the key line, "And we are here," the poet turns back to the girl. "We are here," solidly, constantly, as the seascape was in stanza one; and we are quite distinctly separate from what conflicts with that solid, constant trust—the ignorant armies. They are quite distinctly not "we"; and they are distanced from "we" by "as," that is, by metaphor and literary reference. /18/ The fact that "we are here" stands between the first half of the stanza and the second, preventing the second half from penetrating the first. Paradoxically, as Theodore Morrison pointed out many years ago, the poem uses love precisely to prevent the disillusionment involved in a knowledge of sexuality.[7]

---

[7] "Dover Beach Revisited: A New Fable for Critics," *Harper's Magazine*, CLXXX (1940). "The ordinary degree of aggressiveness, the normal joy of conquest and possession, seemed to be wholly absent from him. The love he asked for was

The strategy of the poem thus consists of four stages. First, the poet gives us a world felt as constant, nurturing, evoking faith. Second, he discovers a disillusioning sound. Third, he rejects the whole thing to get rid of that disillusioning sound. Fourth, he re-treats from his global wishes and tries to re-create the earlier idyllic state in miniature, in a personal relationship. The poem defends by denial; it gets rid of the disillusioning sound by putting it metaphori-cally away from the poet. Then the poem gives pleasure by re-creat-ing an adult world in terms of a child's wishes for constancy, trust, and faith in his parents.[8]

Notice, too, how the poet makes us experience for ourselves the experience the poem describes. He gives us, first, the somewhat vague seascape, evoking in us both a wish to take in more, and a feeling of trust and security. Then he surprises us with the presence of another. We feel a disturbing influence, which the poems tells us is a sound. So it is—the sudden speaking voice of "Come to the window," and we want to know more, to take in more. Instead, the second and third stanzas try to intellectualize and distance the disturbing influence but fail and come back to it, thus building up tension in us. The fourth stanza abandons these earlier attempts to deal with the prob-lem. First, it suddenly retreats from the external world to the smaller world of the lovers; second, it shifts in metaphor from the Dover seascape to the ignorant armies. The fourth stanza gives us the vague hope, "Let us be true"; and, as at the beginning of the poem, we feel trust, security, but also a desire to take in more. But now we learn that the danger, the moving back and /19/ forth, is elsewhere; we take a metaphorical flight in time and space to the plain of Epipolae. The efforts at flight that failed in stanzas two and three succeed in stanza four because "we are here." The phrase is

---

essentially a protective love, sisterly or motherly; in its unavoidable ingredient of passion he felt a constant danger, which repelled and unsettled him" (see pp. 240–241). Professor Morrison offers his insight in the whimsical spirit of a *Pooh Perplex*, but it seems to me sound nevertheless. This essay, by the way, contains the only other psychoanalytic explication of the poem I know.

[8] Like the theme of sight, the form of rejecting or giving up one thing so as to gain another (often a mollified version of the first) occurs over and over again in Arnold's writings. Among the poems that take this form are: "To a Republican Friend, 1848" (both poems), "Religious Isolation," "In Utrumque Paratus," "Ab-sence," "Self-Dependence," "A Summer Night," "The Buried Life," "The Scholar-Gipsy," "Thyrsis," "Rugby Chapel"; and among the prose, "On Translating Homer," "The Function of Criticism at the Present Time," the rejection of Philistinism, anarchy, Hebraism, and so on. "I am fargments," Arnold wrote to "K," and the trope seems to represent a basic defense for him. "Dover Beach" is quintessential Arnold as well as quintessential Victorian.

almost parental; and thus, by the very acceptance of disillusionment, the poem gratifies us, because it does, ultimately, let us take in what we wished to take in: it lets us see two "true" lovers together with a glimpse of a "clash by night" elsewhere.

The poem makes us experience the experience described by the poem, and we can see it does in the various explications. We have spoken of the poem as a re-creating of the child's trust that he will be nurtured, that he will be able to take in and be taken into some comforting environment. Krieger speaks of the poem as "the repetitive *inclusiveness* of the human situation." We have spoken of the poem as an attempt to re-create the world as it once was, in childhood. Krieger speaks of repetitiveness and "the tragic sense of *eternal recurrence.*" We have spoken of the disturbing note in the poem as the sense of ebb and flow that cuts down a child's faith that the nurturing world will always be there. Bonnerot speaks of "the sea-rhythm of the world in general and also of the poet's soul which finds itself mysteriously in accord with that cosmic pulse,"[9] while Delasanta speaks of "terrible incompatibility"—the two sides of a child's trust.

In short, a psychological understanding of the poem as an interaction of impulses and defenses complements conventional explication because it reveals the emotional underpinnings to our objective understanding of the poem. It enables us to speak objectively about our subjective experience of the poem, even when those subjective experiences vary sharply. But what can this kind of awareness of the poem as impulse and defense contribute to literary history?

A preliminary question, though, must be: What do we mean by literary history? Once literary history moves beyond the mere chronicling of names and dates, as in a reference book, we ask, I think, that it /20/ be an attempt to understand literary events historically, that

---

[9] Bonnerot offers a curious confirmation of the reading here suggested, that the sea in "Dover Beach" evokes feelings like those toward a nurturing mother. Immediately after the statement cited, he quotes (free associates to?) the following from *God and the Bible*: "Only when one is young and headstrong can one thus prefer bravado to experience, can one stand by the Sea of Time, and instead of listening to the solemn and rhythmical beat of its waves, choose to fill the air with one's own whoopings to start the echo." It is not too difficult to hear under Arnold's "whoopings" something like a child's anguished howls to prevent his mother's withdrawal or bring her back ("start the echo") or replace the void she leaves ("fill the air"). There is further confirmation in Arnold's letter to Clough of 29 Sept. 1848, where he describes himself as "one who looks upon water as the Mediator between the inanimate and man." See H. F. Lowry, ed., *The Letters of Matthew Arnold to Arthur Hugh Clough* (London, 1932), p. 92.

is, as having causes or meaningful relations to other events in time. Typically, though, when literary history moves from chronicle to history, it shades off into the history of ideas. Literary history, as such, ceases to be a separate discipline. The reason this happens, I think, is that we are accustomed to look at the content of literature when we are looking at literature historically. But content is not what is literary in literature—form is; the kind and quality of expression is. In psychoanalytic terms, form and mode of expression are defenses; and, therefore, to write literary history which is not merely a branch of the history of ideas, literary history which deals with what is literary in literature, we shall have to write about the defenses a particular culture uses. We shall have to think more like a cultural anthropologist that an intellectual historian.

Many critics have said "Dover Beach" is the representative, the quintessential Victorian poem, or, in Krieger's gentle pun, a "highly Victorian" poem. Mostly, however, the critics have said this because they see the poem as primarily about doubt and loss of faith—major themes in Victorian ideas. But "Dover Beach" is an emotional experience, not just an intellectual one. Further, to see the poem as only about doubt is not to see the form of the poem, for Arnold sets his doubt and despair against a sexual situation: this is a poem that tells about two lovers alone at night.[10]

We have seen that "Dover Beach" defends against that situation and adapts it to moral and intellectual pleasure by employing three strategies. First, it avoids looking directly at the lovers by intensely looking at and listening to something else, the sea, the shingle, Sophocles, and so on. Second, the poem places its "you" and "I" between illusion and reality so as to keep up a division or dualism, to prevent certain things from mingling or penetrating. The feeling is that if the negative sound touches the positive sight, one must reject them both. One must either accept the world wholly or reject it wholly. Both these defenses the psychoanalyst would call forms of denial: denying the existence of forbidden things by seeing what they are not; denying compromise or imperfection. Then, third, the poem tries to re-create in the relationship with the lover a simplified, more

---

[10] Thus, I think, Walter Houghton comes closer to the theme of doubt when he reminds us: "For the Victorians, the disagreeable facts were primarily those of sex, and the terrifying truth [of] the state of religion" (*The Victorian Frame of Mind,* 1830–1870 [New Haven, 1957], pp. 413–414). In this section of my paper, I am relying very heavily on Professor Houghton's book. My feeling goes beyond mere indebtedness to sheer gratitude that such an encyclopedic and perceptive book exists.

childish, but more satisfying version of an adult love for another person or the world as a whole. /21/

In short, the psychoanalytic study of this quintessentially Victorian poem cues us to a particular hypothesis as to what makes it so "Victorian": a certain pattern of defenses, namely, the use of denial to recreate an adult world to meet a child's demand for perfection. Now, we need to ask, To what extent is this pattern characteristically Victorian? If it is characteristic, where did it come from? How did it sustain itself? And how is it expressed in literary forms?

Obviously, we cannot answer all these questions in a mere essay, but we can begin. We can begin with the way the Victorian style itself began—with the rejection of the Regency and all the four Georges, the rejection of eighteenth-century club-life and other levities, the rejection of the aristocracy, and the rejection of Byronism and the excesses of Romanticism.[11] Psychologically, such a massive rejection of the past is, at some level of a man's being, a rejection of his parents, his forebears in a physical as well as an intellectual or historical sense. It is no accident, I think, that this age that so rejected immediate parenthood should also have been so preoccupied with the problem of evolution, parenthood distanced to a prehistoric past. Kenneth Burke suggests the characteristic mental habit of the nineteenth century was translating "essence" into "origin" so that the statement, "This is the essence of the situation," becomes "This is how it began."[12] And this strategy, too, I take it, is a way of looking for lost origins—parenthood —in areas safely distanced from real origins.

When the Victorians rejected their immediate past, what did they replace it with? Just as they stuffed and over-stuffed their rooms with furniture, they felt they were creating a new world themselves—and not without reason. "Your railroad," Thackeray could write, "starts the new era." "We are of the age of steam." "It was only yesterday, but what a gulf between now and then!" In a very real sense, the newly powerful middle class could claim to have created itself, psychologically, to have been its own parents or, in Clough's phrase, by its very success to have achieved "This keen supplanting of nearest kin."

But when we look to see how the Victorians thought of parents, we

---

[11] Houghton, pp. 45–53, 109, 300, and 342. Lionel Trilling, "The Fate of Pleasure: Wordsworth to Dostoevsky," in Northrop Frye, ed., *Romanticism Reconsidered: Selected Papers from the English Institute* (New York, 1963), pp. 73–106, particularly pp. 73–90 and 97–101. Professor Trilling's paper develops brilliantly the idea that Victorian moral and spiritual energy should be regarded as an effort to mask over—indeed, attack—pleasures erotic and gentlemanly. My own essay might well be regarded as the attempt to extend Professor Trilling's hypothesis to a particular poem and to literary forms.

[12] Cited by Stanley Edgar Hyman, *The Tangled Bank* (New York, 1962), p. 366.

find that, if the Victorians were their own parents, they were a /22/ rather special kind of parent. Mother becomes Patmore's *Angel in the House,* or, as Tennyson's Prince describes her,

> No angel, but a dearer being, all dipt
> In angel instincts, breathing Paradise,
> Interpreter between the gods and men . . .

As for the gods, we recognize the Victorian father: a man thought of primarily in terms of force and power and authority, a king or hero on Carlyle's model, a captain of industry, almost an Old Testament God. What such parents lack, of course, is adult sexuality, which is replaced by a kind of industrial force or household contentment.

We see the same denial in Victorian hero-worship, particularly of heroes who combined features of a father and a son: wild, primitive figures, but of impeccable moral stature. The favorite was the Galahad story, and it tells us the Victorian secret: the denial of sexuality leads to physical strength or, to put it another way, the Victorians looked at a man's strength as a way of not seeing a man's sexuality. Symbols for the denial are the baptismal images that recur in Victorian writing, of water or cleansing of the soiled self, as in *The Water Babies* or Kingsley's whole advice for life—"hard work and cold water."[13]

What I am suggesting is that the Victorians in general, like Arnold in "Rugby Chapel," sought parents such as a child would wish, parents devoid of sexuality. What the Victorians rejected in their social parents, the eighteenth century, the Regency, they rejected in their actual parents: levity, libertinism, gentlemanly pleasures, sexuality. As Thackeray complained in the preface to *Pendennis,* his readers would not accept a virile man or a realistic woman. When the Victorians created their own new world, became parents themselves, they became parents on this infantile model. Thus, we find Beatrice Webb's father, though he was a railway tycoon, kneeling down morning and night to repeat the prayer he learned at his mother's lap—"Gentle Jesus, meek and mild, look upon a little child." Perhaps it is true of any age baffled by the complexities of rapid change that it regresses, tries to come to grips with its world in more primitive, childish terms; but the Victorians do seem to have done so more than most.

In this wish to re-create one's parents on the model of a child's wishes, we find an answer to what is to me the most puzzling problem of Victorian life: Why was it a stable society? After all, the Victorians tried to put down wit, levity, leisure, acceptance, and passivity, along with sex. It was a stately, solemn, perhaps dreary kind of culture. And

---

[13] Jerome Buckley, *The Victorian Temper* (Cambridge, 1951), pp. 98–105.

/23/ yet it lasted fifty or so years. People must have found some sort of compensating pleasure in it. They found, I think, the granting of one of the strongest and deepest wishes of childhood, a wish that persists with great strength into adult life, namely, the desire to maintain the fantasy that one's parents be sexually pure.

Thus, obliquely, "Dover Beach" has led us to at least a hypothesis about the major Victorian modes of defense. In the terms of intellectual history, Walter Houghton describes them as "a process of deliberately ignoring whatever was unpleasant and pretending it did not exist." In psychoanalytic terms, these defenses are avoidance, denial, suppression, repression—all those defensive strategies summed up in Mr. Podsnap's formulaic, "I don't want to know about it; I don't choose to discuss it; I don't admit it!"

But these defenses have a positive side as well as the merely negative one. They lead to the Victorian effort to remodel the world, to earnestness, enthusiasm, the belief in the basic goodness of human nature, dogmatism, rigidity, an emphasis on doing (Arnold's "Hebraism"), the gospel of intellectual, moral, and social work, the drive and duty to succeed. All are ways of emulating a father conceived of as nonsexual industrial or moral drive; or of gratifying a mother conceived in terms of Ruskin's "Goddess of Getting-on," or what Arnold called "Mrs. Gooch's Golden Rule," her counsel to her son: "My dear Dan . . . you should look forward to being some day manager of that concern!" As for intellectual life, we find generally what Mill described as a "rather more demonstrative attitude of belief" than people thought necessary "when their personal conviction was more complete." We see the Victorian never-ending quest for truth, as though one were constantly trying to find some truth other than the one you have denied and left behind you. At the same time, we find an unwillingness to draw ultimate conclusions, to come to a stopping place lest the intellectual quest end. Thus, too, we find poems like "The Scholar-Gipsy" or Tennyson's "Ulysses" praising aspiration, movement, energy, force without aim or end, for if one came to an end, one might have to sit down and think about what was left behind[14]—"The Buried Life," Arnold called it;

> our own only true, deep-buried selves,
> Being one with which we are one with the whole world.

---

[14] "For the Victorians, intense activity was both a rational method of attacking the anxieties of the time, and an irrational method of escaping them" (Houghton, p. 262). See also Kristian Smidt, "The Intellectual Quest of the Victorian Poets," *English Studies*, XL (1959), 90–102.

For those with eyes less open than Arnold's, the buried life be- /24/ came the dark underside of Victorian optimism: the fear that what was denied might return, and the optimism founded on denial be upset. There might be a revolution from below, from the masses. There might come corruption from abroad, the pernicious writings of, say Balzac or Flaubert, or even the local product, the "fleshly school of poetry." Abstract thought and contemplation are dangerous. Knowledge and love are antithetical, as in Browning's *Paracelsus*. Levity becomes the light treatment of evil. Leisure is thought of as the occasion of all evil. The devil finds work for idle hands—and we can guess at the fear of what idle hands might be doing. These are the anxieties, doubts, and pessimisms that gnaw underneath the superstructure of Victorian optimism, things that a Carlyle or even an Arnold would try to put down by force, George Eliot by a cult of obedience, or Macaulay by a trust in progress.

Doubt and despair followed by a commitment to work backed up by religious or philosophic principle—this is, of course, what Jerome Buckley (ch. v) has called "the pattern of Victorian conversion," and it is well known. What I am suggesting is a psychological paradigm for this Victorian life-style. We could put it this way: I reject my actual forebears (the eighteenth century and its attitudes). I create the world anew. I thus become my own parent, but—and this is the important point—I become a parent such as a child would wish. I deny the adult emotions, sexuality, but also easiness, indifference, the enjoyment of leisure, the tolerance of uncertainty. Instead, I work, I am enthusiastic, I am earnest. And the last steps carry out the first two. I deny the adult emotions and so continue the rejection of what went before. I busy myself and so I create the world anew. The system closes upon itself and becomes the stable, though uneasy, style of the long Victorian calm. It is uneasy because the whole circle rests on a denial that leaves a weak point at which Swinburne and Pater and Meredith and Hardy and Wilde will penetrate the system and break it down.

But what does this say about literary history? Obviously, much of the content of Victorian poetry expresses either the frantic affirmations or the covert doubts of Victorian culture. This is the content, however. What about defenses understood as giving rise to forms and modes of expression? "Dover Beach" cues us to look for three defenses. First, concentrating on one thing as a way of not seeing something else. Second, a tendency to try to keep things from mingling, to divide experience into total acceptance or total rejection, to avoid compromise or the acceptance of imperfection. Third, the re-creation of an adult world according /25/ to a child's wish for perfection, specifically, that his parents be sexually pure. If our hypothesis is correct, these defenses must give rise to at least some of the forms and styles of Victorian literature.

And so, it seems to me, they do. Many critics have pointed to a kind of divided allegiance in Victorian poetry: the poet as a public, social spokesman, but with a buried self; a pervasive dichotomy between social and moral subjects and personal ones. In psychoanalytic terms, we recognize one of the "Dover Beach" defenses, concentrating on one thing so as not to see another, or, as E. D. H. Johnson puts it, "The expressed content has a dark companion."[15] The same defense shows in the way the Victorian poet relies on a natural scene. "Arnold," notes Truss, "typically grafted an idea to a landscape, and he tried to make the landscape do his talking for him." Trilling's phrasing is kinder when he speaks of "Arnold's bold dramatic way of using great objects, often great geographical or topographical objects, in relation to which the subjective states of the poem organize themselves and seem themselves to acquire an objective actuality."[16] The massive landscape takes our attention away from the poet.

Another popular form of the period distances the same way: the dramatic monologue affirms an external reality at the expense of the poet's subjective state (though as Kristian Smidt has shown, the distancing often collapses into an "oblique" or "diagonal" point of view in which the poet blurs into his spokesman—the denial breaks down).[17] Along with the dramatic monologue, we find in criticism a tendency to look at the events described by a work of art rather than at the work of art itself, to treat Shakespearean characters as real people, for example. This, too, enables the Victorian to concentrate on one thing as a way of not seeing something else—his own emotional reaction.

If "Dover Beach" is quintessentially Victorian, we should be able to find in Victorian forms generally the second of its defenses, namely, dividing the world into black and white, yea and nay. Thus, when the

---

[15] E. D. H. Johnson, *The Alien Vision of Victorian Poetry* (Princeton, 1952), p. 217.

[16] Tom J. Truss, "Arnold's 'Shakespeare,'" *Explicator*, XIX (1961), 56. Lionel Trilling, ed., *The Portable Matthew Arnold* (New York, 1949), p. 39. See also Marshall McLuhan, "The Aesthetic Moment in Landscape Poetry," in Alan S. Downer, ed., *English Institute Essays 1951* (New York, 1952), pp. 168–181.

[17] Kristian Smidt, "Point of View in Victorian Poetry," *English Studies*, XXXVIII (1957), 1–12.

Victorian style began, poetic imagery shifted away from the growth and profusion of the Romantics, uniting with the world, to images of polarity and tension, dividing oneself from the world or dividing the world itself, as Arnold does in "Dover Beach" (Johnson, 1961 p. 2). /26/ In this sense, the pervasive dichotomy in Victorian poetry between social and moral subjects and personal ones becomes another way of polarizing the external world created from child-like optimism and the darker, more adult emotions within. Arnold, in particular, came increasingly to feel that a natural or general law proscribed the expression of his own deep feelings[18]—for "general law" we can read the pervasive defense of the man and his culture. Again, we find Victorian poetry heavily committed to poetic diction, a kind of fulfillment of Bentham's view of the arts. Poetic diction serves as a way of distinguishing poetry from normal adult speech, an optimizing of ordinary language, reconstructing it in terms of a wish for perfection— a kind of extremely adult baby-talk.

We can see both these "Dover Beach" defenses, for example, in the pre-Raphaelite style. Both the concentration on visual detail and the heavy use of emblem and allegory serve the Victorian denial much as Arnold's viewing of the seascape does. We look intensely at one thing, at one meaning or sight, and so we avoid seeing something else. Heavy symbolism and allegory; a retreat to Greek, Biblical, medieval, or exotic legend; the ample rendering of visual details—these are present to some extent in all Victorian poetry, but these various overstatements in the service of denial fuse in the pre-Raphaelite style to make it, too, quintessentially Victorian.

But poetry, of course, was not the greatest form in the period. The output may have been vast, but the quality was sharply limited, perhaps because poetry as the expression of personal feelings did not suit an age dedicated to the denial of certain key feelings. The "Spasmodic school" suggests the trouble poets got into when they tried to express feelings directly, unshielded by dramatic monologue or landscape. The novel expressed Victorian needs better, notably, the wish to concentrate on one thing as a way of not seeing another. Just as, on the stage, theatrical spectacle and declamatory acting shifted attention away from the lack of realistic emotion in the characters, so the great shift of the English novel from the eighteenth century to the nineteenth is a growing attention to the larger social environment surrounding the central characters. At the same time, the usual Victorian

---

[18] John M. Wallace, "Landscape and 'The General Law': The Poetry of Matthew Arnold," *Boston University Studies in English*, V (1961), 91–106.

novel offered its readers adult emotions over-simplified and desexualized. The Victorian novel, like Victorian commerce, sought to order the complex adult world by the wishes of a child. As Joseph Schumpeter has shown, in Victorian commerce, the industrialist became paternalistic, a father; /27/ the colonial took on the burdens of his "little brown brother."[19] The larger political and economic world was to be organized in terms of family responsibility. And so the novelist by the form of his novel often suggested—*Bleak House* is the obvious and best example—that the cure for the ills of the adult environment was simply to re-create the family world of a child in the world at large.

The Victorian novel polarized the world into a large environment and a family of central characters, just as Victorian drama polarized its world into elaborate visual spectacle and a star or two. Yet the novel thrived while the drama declined. I think we can understand the decline of the drama as a case in which a genre found itself caught between two Victorian modes of defense. On the one hand, there is the avoidance of one thing by looking at another, giving rise to the interest in visual spectacle and declamatory acting as ways not to see the central characters too realistically. On the other hand, there was the wish to see adult emotions through a child's eyes. Thus, Hazlitt could say of Joanna Baillie, "She treats her grown men as little girls treat their dolls." We can accept what E. M. Forster calls "flat" characters in fiction; we can accept sentimentality, for the novelist can adjust the whole world of the novel to fit his myth, in this case, the re-creation through denial of a world to fit a child's wishes. But sentimentalism is harder to accept when physically set before us on a stage that so insists on physical realities and visual exactness as the Victorian theatre did, indeed as that whole age that invented photography did.

I have not yet mentioned the greatest of all genres in the Victorian period: nonsense, which was the most admirably suited to the Victorian defense strategy. Lear and Carroll offered a reassuring form of humor, one that did not "treat evil lightly," one that was not "levity, insincerity, and idle babble and play-acting" (to give Carlyle's list of sins). Rather, Lear and Carroll did the truly Victorian

---

[19] *Imperialism and Social Classes,* trans. Heinz Norden, ed. Paul M. Sweezy (New York, 1951), pp. 153–159, 169–170, 190–205, and 220–221. Schumpeter's neo-Marxist analysis of the necessity for a family to do something de novo to break the class barrier and his concept of "patrimonialization" strikingly confirm, from the quite alien point of view of economics, the psychoanalytic hypothesis I am advancing about Victorian England.

thing directly: they explicitly re-created the world of an adult through the eyes of a child.

So far, our hypothesis holds. "Dover Beach" cued us to look in Victorian culture and Victorian literary modes for a pattern of defense: /28/ the use of denial to re-create an adult world according to what a child wishes adults would be.[20] Allegory, poetic diction, dramatic monologue, landscape poetry, sentimentality in fiction and spectacle in drama, nonsense—all these forms and styles of Victorian literature we have looked at so far tend to confirm our hypothesis. Whether the hypothesis will stand further testing, time will tell. Obviously, one would have to have many, many more analyses of literary works to prove or disprove it finally. The more general point, though, the methodological one, stands. Psychoanalysis can offer the literary historian a hypothesis, at least, and perhaps even a full understanding of the way literary forms act analogously to defenses to meet the psychological needs of a culture.

I think psychoanalysis can add something else: sympathy. For example, in "Dover Beach" Arnold writes as though he actually expected the world to supply joy, love, light, certitude, peace, help for pain, and I—a creature of the twentieth century—am puzzled. My world has been the depression, World War II, Auschwitz, the cold war—frankly, I expect nothing from my world but trouble. In another sense, though, I can think back, experience back, to a time when my world was smaller and consisted of a mother and a father in a small apartment in New York. Then was a time when I, like Arnold, could expect—and get—joy, love, light, help for pain. And, therefore, despite what batterings that sense of basic trust may have taken, I can enter and experience Arnold's quite alien kind of world. I can love Arnold's poem.

In short, what psychoanalysis can bring to literary history is not only hypotheses about the uses of literary forms. It can also bring sympathy, an ability to call back to life in ourselves the feeling of

---

[20] Obviously, throughout this essay, I have been using the term "Victorian" in a broad, attributive way, as if I were to look at a house or an attitude or a poem and say "That's quite Victorian." The defensive pattern, then, explicates the word. Equally obviously, though, there are many particular Victorianisms: high and low, early, middle, and late, and so on. One could refine the technique developed in this essay by sketching out the kind of thing denoted by the more specific term "high Victorian" and then trying to analyze that kind of thing as analogous to psychological defenses. If this essay is correct, each specific Victorianism should turn out to be a narrower form of the general pattern of impulse and defense here suggested.

writers and ages long gone. The message psychoanalysis sends the literary historian comes down simply to this: if you wish to write the literary history of Victorian England, do not simply seek the Victorian (like Carroll's snark) with forks and hope or names and dates back there. Look for the Victorian in yourself.

Theodore Morrison

Dover Beach Revisited:
A New Fable for Critics*

Early in the year 1939 a certain Professor of Educational Psychology, occupying a well-paid chair at a large endowed university, conceived a plot. From his desk in the imposing Hall of the Social Sciences where the Research Institute in Education was housed he had long burned with resentment against teachers of literature, especially against English departments. It seemed to him that the professors of English stood square across the path of his major professional ambition. His great desire in life was to introduce into the study, the teaching, the critical evaluation of literature some of the systematic method, some of the "objective procedure" as he liked to call it, some of the certainty of result which he believed to be characteristic of the physical sciences. "You make such a fetish of science," a colleague once said to him, "why aren't you a chemist?"—a question that annoyed him deeply.

If such a poem as Milton's "Lycidas" has a value—and most English teachers, even to-day, would start with that as a cardinal fact—then that value must be measurable and expressible in terms that do not shift and change from moment to moment and person to person with every subjective whim. They would agree, these teachers of literature, these professors of English, that the value of the poem is in some sense objective; they would never agree to undertake any objective procedure to determine what that value is. They would not clearly define what they meant by achievement in the study of literature, and they bridled and snorted when anyone else attempted to define it. He remembered what had happened when he had once been

---

* Reprinted from *Harper's Magazine*, CLXXX (February, 1940), 235–44, by special permission. Copyright © 1940, by Harper's Magazine, Inc.

incautious enough to suggest to a professor of English in his own college that it might be possible to establish norms for the appreciation
of Milton. The fellow had simply exploded into a peal of histrionic
laughter and then had tried to wither him with an equally histrionic
look of incredulity and disgust.

He would like to see what would happen if the teachers of English
were forced or lured, by some scheme or other, into a public exposure
of their position. It would put them in the light of intellectual charla-
tanism, nothing less . . . and suddenly Professor Chartly (for so he
was nicknamed) began to see his way.

It was a simple plan that popped into his head, simple yet bold and
practical. It was a challenge that could not be refused. A strategically
placed friend in one of the large educational foundations could be
counted on: there would be money for clerical expenses, for travel if
need be. He took his pipe from his pocket, filled it, and began to puff
exultantly. To-morrow he must broach the scheme to one or two colleagues; to-night, over cheese and beer, would not be too soon. He
reached for the telephone.

The plan that he unfolded to his associates that evening aroused
considerable /236/ skepticism at first, but gradually they succumbed
to his enthusiasm. A number of well-known professors of literature at
representative colleges up and down the land would be asked to write
a critical evaluation of a poem prominent enough to form part of the
standard reading in all large English courses. They would be asked
to state the criteria on which they based their judgment. When all
the answers had been received the whole dossier would be sent to a
moderator, a trusted elder statesman of education, known everywhere
for his dignity, liberality of intelligence, and long experience. He
would be asked to make a preliminary examination of all the documents and to determine from the point of view of a teacher of literature whether they provided any basis for a common understanding.
The moderator would then forward all the documents to Professor
Chartly, who would make what in his own mind he was frank to call
a more scientific analysis. Then the jaws of the trap would be ready
to spring.

Once the conspirators had agreed on their plot their first difficulty
came in the choice of a poem. Suffice it to say that someone eventually
hit on Arnold's "Dover Beach," and the suggestion withstood all attack. "Dover Beach" was universally known, almost universally
praised; it was remote enough so that contemporary jealousies and
cults were not seriously involved, yet near enough not to call for any
special expertness, historical or linguistic, as a prerequisite for judg-

ment; it was generally given credit for skill as a work of art, yet it contained also, in its author's own phrase, a "criticism of life."

Rapidly in the days following the first meeting the representative teachers were chosen and invited to participate in the plan. Professional courtesy seemed to require the inclusion of an Arnold expert. But the one selected excused himself from producing a value judgment of "Dover Beach" on the ground that he was busy investigating a fresh clue to the identity of "Marguerite." He had evidence that the woman in question, after the episode hinted at in the famous poems, had married her deceased sister's husband, thus perhaps affecting Arnold's views on a social question about which he had said a good deal in his prose writings. The expert pointed out that he had been given a half-year's leave of absence and a research grant to pursue the shadow of Marguerite through Europe, wherever it might lead him. If only war did not break out he hoped to complete this research and solve one of the vexing problems that had always confronted Arnold's biographers. His energies would be too much engaged in this special investigation to deal justly with the more general questions raised by Professor Chartly's invitation. But he asked to be kept informed, since the results of the experiment could not fail to be of interest to him.

After a few hitches and delays from other quarters, the scheme was ripe. The requests were mailed out, and the Professor of Educational Psychology sat back in grim confidence to await the outcome.

II

It chanced that the first of the representative teachers who received and answered Professor Chartly's letter was thought of on his own campus as giving off a distinct though not unpleasant odor of the ivory tower. He would have resented the imputation himself. At forty-five Bradley Dewing was handsome in a somewhat speciously virile style, graying at the temples, but still well-knit and active. He prided himself on being able to beat most of his students at tennis; once a year he would play the third or fourth man on the varsity and go down to creditable defeat with some elegiac phrases on the ravages of time. He thought of himself as a man of the world; it was well for his contentment, which was seldom visibly ruffled, that he never heard the class mimic reproducing at a fraternity house or beer parlor his man- /237/ ner of saying: "After all, gentlemen, it is pure poetry that lasts. We must never forget the staying power of pure art." The class mimic never represents the whole of class opinion but he can usually make everyone within earshot laugh.

Professor Dewing could remember clearly what his own teachers had said about "Dover Beach" in the days when he was a freshman in college himself, phrases rounded with distant professorial unction: faith and doubt in the Victorian era; disturbing influence of Darwin on religious belief; Browning the optimist; Tennyson coming up with firm faith after a long struggle in the waters of doubt; Matthew Arnold, prophet of skepticism. How would "Dover Beach" stack up now as a poem? Pull Arnold down from the shelf and find out.

Ah, yes, how the familiar phrases came back. The sea is calm, the tide is full, the cliffs of England stand . . . And then the lines he particularly liked:

> Come to the window, sweet is the night air!
> Only, from the long line of spray
> Where the ebb meets the moon-blanch'd sand,
> Listen! you hear the grating roar
> Of pebbles which the waves draw back, and fling,
> At their return, up the high strand,
> Begin, and cease, and then again begin,
> With tremulous cadence slow . . .

Good poetry, that! No one could mistake it. Onomatopoeia was a relatively cheap effect most of the time. Poe, for instance: "And the silken sad uncertain rustling of each purple curtain." Anyone could put a string of s's together and make them rustle. But these lines in "Dover Beach" were different. The onomatopoeia was involved in the whole scene, and it in turn involved the whole rhythmical movement of the verse, not the mere noise made by the consonants or vowels as such. The pauses—only, listen, draw back, fling, begin, cease—how they infused a subdued melancholy into the moonlit panorama at the same time that they gave it the utmost physical reality by suggesting the endless iteration of the waves! And then the phrase "With tremulous cadence slow" coming as yet one more touch, one "fine excess," when it seemed that every phrase and pause the scene could bear had already been lavished on it: that was Miltonic, Virgilian.

But the rest of the poem?

> The sea of Faith
> Was once, too, at the full, and round earth's shore
> Lay like the folds of a bright girdle furl'd . . .

Of course Arnold had evoked the whole scene only to bring before us this metaphor of faith in its ebb-tide. But that did not save the figure from triteness and from an even more fatal vagueness. Everything in second-rate poetry is compared to the sea: love is as deep, grief as salty, passion as turbulent. The sea may look like a bright girdle sometimes, though Professor Dewing did not think it particularly impressive to say so. And in what sense is *faith* a bright girdle? Is it the function of faith to embrace, to bind, to hold up a petticoat, or what? And what is the faith that Arnold has in mind? The poet evokes no precise concept of it. He throws us the simple, undifferentiated word, unites its loose emotional connotations with those of the sea, and leaves the whole matter there. And the concluding figure of "Dover Beach":

> we are here as on a darkling plain
> Swept with confused alarms of struggle and flight,
> Where ignorant armies clash by night.

Splendid in itself, this memorable image. But the sea had been forgotten now; the darkling plain had displaced the figure from which the whole poem tacitly promised to evolve. It would not have been so if John Donne had been the craftsman. A single bold yet accurate analogy, with constantly developing implications, would have served him for the whole poem.

Thus mused Professor Dewing, the lines of his verdict taking shape in his head. A critic of poetry of course was not at liberty to pass judgment on a poet's thought; he could only judge /238/ whether, in treating of the thought or sensibility he had received from his age, the poet had produced a satisfactory work of art. Arnold, Professor Dewing felt, had not been able to escape from the didactic tone or from a certain commonness and vagueness of expression. With deep personal misgivings about his position, in a world both socially and spiritually barbarous, he had sought an image for his emotion, and had found it in the sea—a natural phenomenon still obscured by the drapings of conventional beauty and used by all manner of poets to express all manner of feelings. "Dover Beach" would always remain notable, Professor Dewing decided, as an expression of Victorian sensibility. It contained lines of ever memorable poetic skill. But it could not, he felt, be accepted as a uniformly satisfactory example of poetic art.

III

It was occasionally a source of wonder to those about him just why Professor Oliver Twitchell spent so much time and eloquence urging that man's lower nature must be repressed, his animal instincts kept in bounds by the exertion of the higher will. To the casual observer, Professor Twitchell himself did not seem to possess much animal nature. It seemed incredible that a desperate struggle with powerful bestial passions might be going on at any moment within his own slight frame, behind his delicate white face in which the most prominent feature was the octagonal glasses that focused his eyes on the outside world. Professor Twitchell was a good deal given to discipleship but not much to friendship. He had himself been a disciple of the great Irving Babbitt, and he attracted a small number of disciples among his own more earnest students. But no one knew him well. Only one of his colleagues, who took a somewhat sardonic interest in the mysteries of human nature, possessed a possible clue to the origin of his efforts to repress man's lower nature and vindicate his higher. This colleague had wormed his way sufficiently into Oliver Twitchell's confidence to learn about his family, which he did not often mention. Professor Twitchell, it turned out, had come of decidedly unacademic stock. One of his brothers was the chief salesman for a company that made domestic fire-alarm appliances. At a moment's notice he would whip out a sample from his bag or pocket, plug it into the nearest electric outlet, and while the bystanders waited in terrified suspense, would explain that in the dead of night, if the house caught fire, the thing would go off with a whoop loud enough to warn the soundest sleeper. Lined up with his whole string of brothers and sisters, all older than he, all abounding in spirits, Professor Twitchell looked like the runt of the litter. His colleague decided that he must have had a very hard childhood, and that it was not his own animal nature that he needed so constantly to repress, but his family's.

Whatever the reasons, Professor Twitchell felt no reality in the teaching of literature except as he could extract from it definitions and illustrations of man's moral struggle in the world. For him recent history had been a history of intellectual confusion and degradation, and hence of social confusion and degradation. Western thought had fallen into a heresy. It had failed to maintain the fundamental grounds of a true humanism. It had blurred the distinction between man, God, and nature. Under the influence of the sciences, it had set up a monism in which the moral as well as the physical constitution of man was included within nature and the laws of nature. It had, therefore, exalted man as naturally good, and exalted the free expression of all his impulses. What were the results of this heresy? An age, complained Professor Twitchell bitterly, in which young women talked about sexual perversions at the dinner table; an age in which everyone agreed that society was in dis- /239/ solution and insisted on the privilege of being dissolute; an age without any common standards of value in morals or art; an age, in short, without discipline, without self-restraint in private life or public.

Oliver Twitchell when he received Professor Chartly's envelope sat down with a strong favorable predisposition toward his task. He accepted wholeheartedly Arnold's attitude toward literature: the demand that poetry should be serious, that it should present us with a criticism of life, that it should be measured by standards not merely personal, but in some sense *real.*

"Dover Beach" had become Arnold's best-known poem, admired as his masterpiece. It would surely contain, therefore, a distillation of his attitude. Professor Twitchell pulled down his copy of Arnold and began to read; and as he read he felt himself overtaken by surprised misgiving. The poem began well enough. The allusion to Sophocles, who had heard the sound of the retreating tide by the Ægean centuries ago, admirably prepared the groundwork of high seriousness for a poem which would culminate in a real criticism of human experience. But did the poem so culminate? It was true that the world

> Hath really neither joy, nor love, nor light,
> Nor certitude, nor peace, nor help for pain

if one meant the world as the worldling knows it, the man who conducts his life by unreflective natural impulse. Such a man will soon enough encounter the disappointments of ambition, the instability of all bonds and ties founded on nothing firmer than passion or self-interest. But this incertitude of the world, to a true disciple of culture, should become a means of self-discipline. It should lead him to ask how life may be purified and ennobled, how we may by wisdom and self-restraint oppose to the accidents of the world a true human culture based on the exertion of a higher will. No call to such a positive moral will, Professor Twitchell reluctantly discovered, can be heard in "Dover Beach." Man is an ignorant soldier struggling confusedly in a blind battle. Was this the culminating truth that Arnold the poet had given men in his masterpiece? Professor Twitchell sadly revised his value-judgment of the poem. He could not feel that in his most widely admired performance Arnold had seen life steadily or seen it whole; rather he had seen it only on its worldly side, and seen it under an aspect of terror. "Dover Beach" would always be justly respected for its poetic art, but the famous lines on Sophocles better exemplified the poet as a critic of life.

IV

As a novelist still referred to in his late thirties as "young" and "promising," Rudolph Mole found himself in a curious relation toward his academic colleagues. He wrote for the public, not for the learned journals; hence he was spared the necessity of becoming a pedant. At the same time the more lucrative fruits of pedantry were denied to him by his quiet exclusion from the guild. Younger men sweating for promotion, living in shabby genteel poverty on yearly appointments, their childless wives mimicking their academic shop-talk in bluestocking phrases, would look up from the stacks of five-by-three cards on which they were constantly accumulating notes and references, and would say to him, "You don't realize how lucky you are, teaching composition. You aren't expected to know anything." Sometimes an older colleague, who had passed through several stages of the mysteries of preferment, would belittle professional scholarship to him with an elaborate show of graciousness and envy. "We are all just pedants," he would say. "You teach the students what they really want and need." Rudolph noticed that the self-confessed pedant went busily on publishing monographs and being promoted, while he him-self remained, year by year, the English Department's most eminent poor relation. /240/

He was not embittered. His dealings with students were pleasant and interesting. There was a sense of reality and purpose in trying to elicit from them a better expression of their thoughts, trying to in-crease their understanding of the literary crafts. He could attack their minds on any front he choose, and he could follow his intellectual hobbies as freely as he liked, without being confined to the artificial boundaries of a professional field of learning.

Freud, for example. When Professor Chartly and his accomplices decided that a teacher of creative writing should be included in their scheme and chose Rudolph Mole for the post, they happened to catch him at the height of his enthusiasm for Freud. Not that he expected to psychoanalyze authors through their works; that, he avowed, was not his purpose. You can't deduce the specific secrets of a man's life, he would cheerfully admit, by trying to fit his works into the text-book patterns of complexes and psychoses. The critic, in any case, is in-terested only in the man to the extent that he is involved in his work. But everyone agrees, Rudolph maintained, that the man is involved in his work. Some part of the psychic constitution of the author finds expression in every line that he writes. We can't understand the work unless we can understand the psychic traits that have gained expression in it. We may never be able to trace back these traits to their ultimate sources and causes, probably buried deep in the author's childhood. But we need to gain as much light on them as we can, since they appear in the work we are trying to apprehend, and determine its character. This is what criticism has always sought to do. Freud simply brings new light to the old task.

Rudolph was fortunate enough at the outset to pick up at the college bookstore a copy of Mr. Lionel Trilling's recent study of Matthew Arnold. In this volume he found much of his work already done for him. A footnote to Mr. Trilling's text, citing evidence from Professors Tinker and Lowry, made it clear that "Dover Beach" may well have been written in 1850, some seventeen years before it was first published. This, for Rudolph's purposes, was a priceless discovery. It meant that all the traditional talk about the poem was largely null and void. The poem was not a repercussion of the bombshell that Darwin dropped on the religious sensibilities of the Victorians. It was far more deeply personal and individual than that. Perhaps when Arnold published it his own sense of what it expressed or how it would be understood had changed. But clearly the poem came into being as an expression of what Arnold felt to be the particular kind of affection and passion he needed from a woman. It was a love poem, and took its place with utmost naturalness, once the clue had been given, in the group of similar and related poems addressed to "Marguerite." Mr. Trilling summed up in a fine sentence one strain in these poems, and the principal strain in "Dover Beach," when he wrote that for Arnold "fidelity is a word relevant only to those lovers who see the world as a place of sorrow and in their common suffering require the comfort of constancy."

> Ah, love, let us be true
> To one another! for the world . . .
> Hath really neither joy, nor love, nor light . . .

The point was unmistakable. And from the whole group of poems to which "Dover Beach" belonged, a sketch of Arnold as an erotic personality could be derived. The question whether a "real Marguerite" existed was an idle one, for the traits that found expression in the poems were at least "real" enough to produce the poems and to determine their character.

And what an odd spectacle it made, the self-expressed character of Arnold as a lover! The ordinary degree of aggressiveness, the normal joy of conquest and possession, seemed to be wholly absent from him.

The love he asked for was essentially a protective love, sisterly or
/241/ motherly; in its unavoidable ingredient of passion he felt a
constant danger, which repelled and unsettled him. He addressed
Marguerite as "My sister!" He avowed and deplored his own woman-
ish fits of instability:

> I too have wish'd, no woman more,
> This starting, feverish heart, away.

He emphasized his nervous anguish and contrary impulses. He was a
"teas'd o'erlabour'd heart," "an aimless unallay'd Desire." He could
not break through his fundamental isolation and submerge himself
in another human soul, and he believed that all men shared this
plight:

> Yes: in the sea of life enisl'd,
> With echoing straits between us thrown,
> Dotting the shoreless watery wild,
> We mortal millions live *alone*.

He never "without remorse" allowed himself

> To haunt the place where passions reign,

yet it was clear that whether he had ever succeeded in giving himself
up wholeheartedly to a passion, he had wanted to. There could hardly
be a more telltale phrase than "Once-long'd-for storms of love."

In short much more illumination fell on "Dover Beach" from
certain other verses of Arnold's than from Darwin and all his commentators:

> Truth—what is truth? Two bleeding hearts
> Wounded by men, by Fortune tried,
> Outwearied with their lonely parts,
> Vow to beat henceforth side by side.
>
> The world to them was stern and drear;
> Their lot was but to weep and moan.
> Ah, let them keep their faith sincere,
> For neither could subsist alone!

Here was the nub. "Dover Beach" grew directly from and repeated
the same emotion, but no doubt generalized and enlarged this emotion, sweeping into one intense and far-reaching conviction of insecurity not only Arnold's personal fortunes in love, but the social and

religious faith of the world he lived in. That much could be said for the traditional interpretation.

Of course, as Mr. Trilling did not fail to mention, anguished love affairs, harassed by mysterious inner incompatibilities, formed a well-established literary convention. But the fundamental sense of insecurity in "Dover Beach" was too genuine, too often repeated in other works, to be written off altogether to that account. The same sense of insecurity, the same need for some rock of protection, cried out again and again, not merely in Arnold's love poems but in his elegies, reflective pieces, and fragments of epic as well. Whenever Arnold produced a genuine and striking burst of poetry, with the stamp of true self-expression on it, he seemed always to be in the dumps. Everywhere dejection, confusion, weakness, contention of soul. No adequate cause could be found in the events of Arnold's life for such an acute sense of incertitude; it must have been of psychic origin. Only in one line of effort this fundamental insecurity did not hamper, sadden, or depress him, and that was in the free play of his intelligence as a critic of letters and society. Even there, if it did not hamper his efforts, it directed them. Arnold valiantly tried to erect a barrier of culture against the chaos and squalor of society, against the contentiousness of men. What was this barrier but an elaborate protective device?

The origin of the psychic pattern that expressed itself in Arnold's poems could probably never be discovered. No doubt the influence that Arnold's father exercised over his emotions and his thinking, even though Arnold rebelled to the extent at least of casting off his father's religious beliefs, was of great importance. But much more would have to be known to give a definite clue—more than ever could be known. Arnold was secure from any attempt to spy out the heart of his mystery. But if criticism could not discover the cause, it could assess the result, and could do so (thought Rudolph Mole) with greater understanding by an attempt, with up-to-date psychological aid, to delve a little deeper into the es- /242/ sential traits that manifested themselves in that result.

V

In 1917 Reuben Hale, a young instructor in a Western college, had lost his job and done time in the penitentiary for speaking against conscription and for organizing pacifist demonstrations. In the twenties he had lost two more academic posts for his sympathies with Soviet Russia and his inability to forget his Marxist principles while teaching literature. His contentious, eager, lovable, exasperating temperament tried the patience of one college administration after another. As he advanced into middle age, and his growing family suffered repeated upheavals, his friends began to fear that his robust quarrels with established order would leave him a penniless outcast at fifty. Then he was invited to take a flattering post at a girls' college known for its liberality of views. The connection proved surprisingly durable: in fact it became Professor Hale's turn to be apprehensive. He began to be morally alarmed at his own security, to fear that the bourgeois system which he had attacked so valiantly had somehow outwitted him and betrayed him into allegiance. When the C.I.O. made its initial drive and seemed to be carrying everything before it, he did his best to unseat himself again by rushing joyfully to the nearest picket lines and getting himself photographed by an alert press. Even this expedient failed, and he reconciled himself, not without wonder, to apparent academic permanence.

On winter afternoons his voice could be heard booming out through the closed door of his study to girls who came to consult him on all manner of subjects, from the merits of Plekhanov as a Marxist critic to their own most personal dilemmas. They called him Ben; he called them Smith, Jones, and Robinson. He never relaxed his cheerful bombardment of the milieu into which they were born, and of the larger social structure which made bourgeois wealth, bourgeois art, morals, and religion possible. But when a sophomore found herself pregnant it was to Professor Hale that she came for advice. Should she have an abortion or go through with it and heroically bear the social stigma? And it was Professor Hale who kept the affair from the Dean's office and the newspapers, sought out the boy, persuaded the young couple that they were desperately in love with each other, and that pending the revolution a respectable marriage would be the most prudent course, not to say the happiest.

James Joyce remarks of one of his characters that she dealt with moral problems as a cleaver deals with meat. Professor Hale's critical methods were comparably simple and direct. Literature, like the other arts, is in form and substance a product of society, and reflects the structure of society. The structure of society is a class structure: it is conditioned by the mode of production of goods, and by the legal conventions of ownership and control by which the ruling class keeps itself in power and endows itself with the necessary freedom to exploit men and materials for profit. A healthy literature, in a society so constituted, can exist only if writers perceive the essential economic problem and ally themselves firmly with the working class.

Anyone could see the trouble with Arnold. His intelligence revealed to him the chaos that disrupted the society about him; the selfishness and brutality of the ruling class; the ugliness of the world which the industrial revolution had created, and which imperialism and "liberalism" were extending. Arnold was at his best in his critical satire of this world and of the ignorance of those who governed it. But his intelligence far outran his will, and his defect of will finally blinded his intelligence. He was too much a child of his class to disown it and fight his way to a workable remedy for social injustice. He caught a true vision of himself and of his times as standing between "two worlds, one /243/ dead, one powerless to be born." But he had not courage or stomach enough to lend his own powers to the birth struggle. Had he thrown in his sympathies unreservedly with the working class, and labored for the inescapable revolution, "Dover Beach" would not have ended in pessimism and confusion. It would have ended in a cheerful, strenuous, and hopeful call to action. But Arnold could not divorce himself from the world of polite letters, of education, of culture, into which he had been born. He did his best to purify them, to make them into an instrument for the reform of society. But instinctively he knew that "culture" as he understood the term was not a social force in the world around him. Instinctively he knew that what he loved was doomed to defeat. And so "Dover Beach" ended in a futile plea for protection against the hideousness of the darkling plain and the confused alarms of struggle and flight.

Professor Chartly's envelope brought Reuben Hale his best opportunity since the first C.I.O. picket lines to vindicate his critical and social principles. He plunged into his answer with complete zest.

VI

When Peter Lee Prampton agreed to act as moderator in Professor Chartly's experiment he congratulated himself that this would be his last great academic chore. He had enjoyed his career of scholarship and teaching, no man ever more keenly. But now it was drawing to an end. He was loaded with honors from two continents. The universities of Germany, France, and Britain had first laid their formative hands on his learning and cultivation, then given their most coveted recognition to its fruits. But the honor and the glory seemed a little vague on the June morning when the expressman brought into his library the sizable package of papers which Professor Chartly had boxed and shipped to him. He had kept all his life a certain simplicity of heart. At seventy-four he could still tote a pack with an easy endurance that humiliated men of forty. Now he found himself giving in more and more completely to a lust for trout. Half a century of

hastily snatched vacations in Cape Breton or the Scottish Highlands
had never allowed him really to fill up that hollow craving to find
a wild stream and fish it which would sometimes rise in his throat
even in the midst of a lecture.

Well, there would be time left before he died. And meanwhile here
was this business of "Dover Beach." Matthew Arnold during one of
his American lecture tours had been entertained by neighbors of the
Pramptons. Peter Lee Prampton's father had dined with the great
man, and had repeated his conversation and imitated his accent at the
family table. Peter himself, as a boy of nineteen or so, had gone to
hear Arnold lecture. That, he thought with a smile, was probably a
good deal more than could be said for any of these poor hacks who
had taken Professor Chartly's bait.

At the thought of Arnold he could still hear the carriage wheels
grate on the pebbly road as he had driven, fifty odd years ago, to the
lecture in town, the prospective Mrs. Prampton beside him. His fishing
rod lay under the seat. He chuckled out loud as he remembered how
a pound-and-a-half trout had jumped in the pool under the clattering
planks of a bridge, and how he had pulled up the horse, jumped out,
and tried a cast while Miss Osgood sat scolding in the carriage and
shivering in the autumn air. They had been just a little late reaching
the lecture, but the trout, wrapped in damp leaves, lay safely beside
the rod.

It was queer that "Dover Beach" had not come more recently into
his mind. Now that he turned his thoughts in that direction the poem
was there in its entirety, waiting to be put on again like a coat that
one has worn many times with pleasure and accidentally neglected for
a while.

> The sea of faith was once, too, at the full. /244/

How those old Victorian battles had raged about the Prampton
table when he was a boy! How the names of Arnold, Huxley, Darwin,
Carlyle, Morris, Ruskin had been pelted back and forth by the excited
disputants! *Literature and Dogma, God and the Bible, Culture and
Anarchy*. The familiar titles brought an odd image into his mind: the
tall figure of his father stretching up to turn on the gas lamps in the
evening as the family sat down to dinner; the terrific pop of the pilot
light as it exploded into a net of white flame, shaped like a little
beehive; the buzz and whine of a jet turned up too high.

> Ah, love, let us be true
> To one another! for the world, which seems
> To lie before us like a land of dreams,

So various, so beautiful, so new,
Hath really neither joy, nor love, nor light,
Nor certitude, nor peace, nor help for pain . . .

Peter Lee Prampton shivered in the warmth of his sunny library, shivered with that flash of perception into the past which sometimes enables a man to see how all that has happened in his life, for good or ill, turned on the narrowest edge of chance. He lived again in the world of dreams that his own youth had spread before him, a world truly various, beautiful, and new; full of promise, adventure, and liberty of choice, based on the opportunities which his father's wealth provided, and holding out the prospect of a smooth advance into a distinguished career. Then, within six months, a lavish demonstration that the world has neither certitude, nor peace, nor help for pain: his mother's death by cancer, his father's financial overthrow and suicide, the ruin of his own smooth hopes and the prospect instead of a long, hampered, and obscure fight toward his perhaps impossible ambition. He lived again through the night hours when he had tramped out with himself the youthful question whether he could hold Miss Osgood to her promise in the face of such reversals. And he did not forget how she took his long-sleepless face between her hands, kissed him, and smiled away his anxiety with unsteady lips. Surely everyone discovers at some time or other that the world is not a place of certitude; surely everyone cries out to some other human being for the fidelity which alone can make it so. What more could be asked of a poet than to take so profound and universal an experience and turn it into lines that could still speak long after he and his age were dead?

The best of it was that no one could miss the human feeling, the cry from the heart, in "Dover Beach"; it spoke so clearly and eloquently, in a language everyone could understand, in a form classically pure and simple. Or did it? Who could tell what any job-lot of academicians might be trusted to see or fail to see? And this assortment in Chartly's package might be a queer kettle of fish! Peter Lee Prampton had lived through the *Yellow Book* days of Art for Art's sake; he had read the muckrakers, and watched the rise of the Marxists and the Freudians. Could "Dover Beach" be condemned as unsympathetic with labor? Could a neurosis or a complex be discovered in it? His heart sank at the sharp sudden conviction that indeed these and worse discoveries about the poem might be seriously advanced. Well, he had always tried to go on the principle that every school of criticism should be free to exercise any sincere claim on men's interest and attention which it could win for itself. When he actually applied himself

to the contents of Professor Chartly's bale he would be as charitable
as he could, as receptive to light from any quarter as he could bring
himself to be.

But the task could wait. He felt the need of a period of adjustment
before he could approach it with reasonable equanimity. And in the
meanwhile he could indulge himself in some long-needed editorial
work on his dry-fly book.

William Wordsworth

Lines, Composed a Few Miles above Tintern Abbey, on Revisiting the Banks of the Wye during a Tour. July 13, 1798.

Five years have past; five summers, with the length
Of five long winters! and again I hear
These waters, rolling from their mountain-springs
With a soft inland murmur.—Once again
Do I behold these steep and lofty cliffs,   5
That on a wild secluded scene impress
Thoughts of more deep seclusion; and connect
The landscape with the quiet of the sky.
The day is come when I again repose
Here, under this dark sycamore, and view   10
These plots of cottage-ground, these orchard-tufts,
Which at this season, with their unripe fruits,
Are clad in one green hue, and lose themselves
'Mid groves and copses. Once again I see
These hedge-rows, hardly hedge-rows, little lines   15
Of sportive wood run wild: these pastoral farms,
Green to the very door: and wreaths of smoke
Sent up, in silence, from among the trees!
With some uncertain notice, as might seem
Of vagrant dwellers in the houseless woods,   20
Or of some Hermit's cave, where by his fire
The Hermit sits alone.

                  These beauteous forms,
Through a long absence, have not been to me
As is a landscape to a blind man's eye:
But oft, in lonely rooms, and 'mid the din   25
Of towns and cities, I have owed to them
In hours of weariness, sensations sweet,
Felt in the blood, and felt along the heart;
And passing even into my purer mind,
With tranquil restoration:—feelings too   30
Of unremembered pleasure: such, perhaps,
As have no slight or trivial influence
On that best portion of a good man's life,
His little, nameless, unremembered, acts

Of kindness and of love. Nor less, I trust,   35
To them I may have owed another gift,
Of aspect more sublime; that blessed mood
In which the burthen of the mystery,
In which the heavy and the weary weight
Of all this unintelligible world,   40
Is lightened:—that serene and blessed mood,
In which the affections gently lead us on,—
Until, the breath of this corporeal frame
And even the motion of our human blood
Almost suspended, we are laid asleep   45
In body, and become a living soul:
While with an eye made quiet by the power
Of harmony, and the deep power of joy,
We see into the life of things.
                              If this
Be but a vain belief, yet, oh! how oft—   50
In darkness and amid the many shapes
Of joyless daylight; when the fretful stir
Unprofitable, and the fever of the world,
Have hung upon the beatings of my heart—
How oft, in spirit, have I turned to thee,   55
O sylvan Wye! thou wanderer thro' the woods,
How often has my spirit turned to thee!

    And now, with gleams of half-extinguished thought,
With many recognitions dim and faint,
And somewhat of a sad perplexity,   60
The picture of the mind revives again:
While here I stand, not only with the sense
Of present pleasure, but with pleasing thoughts
That in this moment there is life and food
For future years. And so I dare to hope,   65
Though changed, no doubt, from what I was when first
I came among these hills; when like a roe
I bounded o'er the mountains, by the sides
Of the deep rivers, and the lonely streams,
Wherever nature led: more like a man   70
Flying from something that he dreads than one
Who sought the thing he loved. For nature then
(The coarser pleasures of my boyish days,
And their glad animal movements all gone by)
To me was all in all.—I cannot paint   75

What then I was. The sounding cataract
Haunted me like a passion: the tall rock,
The mountain, and the deep and gloomy wood,
Their colours and their forms, were then to me
An appetite; a feeling and a love,   80
That had no need of a remoter charm,
By thought supplied, nor any interest
Unborrowed from the eye.—That time is past,
And all its aching joys are now no more,
And all its dizzy raptures. Not for this   85
Faint I, nor mourn nor murmur; other gifts
Have followed; for such loss, I would believe,
Abundant recompense. For I have learned
To look on nature, not as in the hour
Of thoughtless youth; but hearing oftentimes   90
The still, sad music of humanity,
Nor harsh nor grating, though of ample power
To chasten and subdue. And I have felt
A presence that disturbs me with the joy
Of elevated thoughts; a sense sublime   95
Of something far more deeply interfused,
Whose dwelling is the light of setting suns,
And the round ocean and the living air,
And the blue sky, and in the mind of man:
A motion and a spirit, that impels   100
All thinking things, all objects of all thought,
And rolls through all things. Therefore am I still
A lover of the meadows and the woods,
And mountains; and of all that we behold
From this green earth; of all the mighty world   105
Of eye, and ear,—both what they half create,
And what perceive; well pleased to recognise
In nature and the language of the sense
The anchor of my purest thoughts, the nurse,
The guide, the guardian of my heart, and soul   110
Of all my moral being.
                  Nor perchance,
If I were not thus taught, should I the more
Suffer my genial spirits to decay:
For thou art with me here upon the banks
Of this fair river; thou my dearest Friend,   115
My dear, dear Friend; and in thy voice I catch

The language of my former heart, and read
My former pleasures in the shooting lights
Of thy wild eyes. Oh! yet a little while
May I behold in thee what I was once,   120
My dear, dear Sister! and this prayer I make
Knowing that Nature never did betray
The heart that loved her; 'tis her privilege,
Through all the years of this our life, to lead
From joy to joy: for she can so inform   125
The mind that is within us, so impress
With quietness and beauty, and so feed
With lofty thoughts, that neither evil tongues,
Rash judgments, nor the sneers of selfish men,
Nor greetings where no kindness is, nor all   130
The dreary intercourse of daily life,
Shall e'er prevail against us, or disturb
Our cheerful faith, that all which we behold
Is full of blessings. Therefore let the moon
Shine on thee in thy solitary walk;   135
And let the misty mountain-winds be free
To blow against thee; and, in after years,
When these wild ecstasies shall be matured
Into a sober pleasure; when thy mind
Shall be a mansion for all lovely forms,   140
Thy memory be as a dwelling-place
For all sweet sounds and harmonies; oh! then,
If solitude, or fear, or pain, or grief,
Should be thy portion, with what healing thoughts
Of tender joy wilt thou remember me,   145
And these my exhortations! Nor, perchance—
If I should be where I no more can hear
Thy voice, nor catch from thy wild eyes these gleams
Of past existence—wilt thou then forget
That on the banks of this delightful stream   150
We stood together; and that I, so long
A worshipper of Nature, hither came
Unwearied in that service: rather say
With warmer love—oh! with far deeper zeal
Of holier love. Nor wilt thou then forget,   155
That after many wanderings, many years
Of absence, these steep woods and lofty cliffs,
And this green pastoral landscape, were to me
More dear, both for themselves and for thy sake!

William Wordsworth

September, 1802. Near Dover.

Inland, within a hollow vale, I stood;
And saw, while sea was calm and air was clear,
The coast of France—the coast of France how near!
Drawn almost into frightful neighbourhood.
I shrunk; for verily the barrier flood
Was like a lake, or river bright and fair,
A span of waters; yet what power is there!
What mightiness for evil and for good!
Even so doth God protect us if we be
Virtuous and wise. Winds blow, and waters roll,
Strength to the brave, and Power, and Deity;
Yet in themselves are nothing! One decree
Spake laws to *them*, and said that by the soul
Only, the Nations shall be great and free.

"It Is a Beauteous Evening..."

It is a beauteous evening, calm and free,
The holy time is quiet as a Nun
Breathless with adoration; the broad sun
Is sinking down in its tranquillity;
The gentleness of heaven broods o'er the Sea:
Listen! the mighty Being is awake,
And doth with his eternal motion make
A sound like thunder—everlastingly.
Dear Child! dear Girl! that walkest with me here,
If thou appear untouched by solemn thought,
Thy nature is not therefore less divine:
Thou liest in Abraham's bosom all the year;
And worshipp'st at the Temple's inner shrine,
God being with thee when we know it not.

141

Archibald MacLeish

"Dover Beach"–
A Note to That Poem

The wave withdrawing
Withers with seaward rustle of flimsy water
Sucking the sand down, dragging at empty shells.
The roil after it settling, too smooth, smothered . . .

After forty a man's a fool to wait in the
Sea's face for the full force and the roaring of
Surf to come over him: droves of careening water.
After forty the tug's out and the salt and the
Sea follow it: less sound and violence.
Nevertheless the ebb has its own beauty—
Shells sand and all and the whispering rustle.
There's earth in it then and the bubbles of foam gone.

Moreover—and this too has its lovely uses—
It's the outward wave that spills the inward forward
Tripping the proud piled mute virginal
Mountain of water in wallowing welter of light and
Sound enough—thunder for miles back. It's a fine and a
Wild smother to vanish in: pulling down—
Tripping with outward ebb the urgent inward.

Speaking alone for myself it's the steep hill and the
Toppling lift of the young men I am toward now,
Waiting for that as the wave for the next wave.
Let them go over us all I say with the thunder of
What's to be next in the world. It's we will be under it!

---

* Reprinted from *Collected Poems: 1917–1952*. Copyright 1952 by Archibald Mac-Leish. Boston: Houghton Mifflin Co., 1952, p. 111, by permission of the publisher.

Anthony Hecht

The Dover Bitch

A Criticism of Life
(for Andrews Wanning)

So there stood Matthew Arnold and this girl
With the cliffs of England crumbling away behind them,
And he said to her, "Try to be true to me,
And I'll do the same for you, for things are bad
All over, etc., etc."
Well now, I knew this girl. It's true she had read
Sophocles in a fairly good translation
And caught that bitter allusion to the sea,
But all the time he was talking she had in mind
The notion of what his whiskers would feel like
On the back of her neck. She told me later on
That after a while she got to looking out
At the lights across the channel, and really felt sad,
Thinking of all the wine and enormous beds
And blandishments in French and the perfumes.
And then she got really angry. To have been brought
All the way down from London, and then be addressed
As a sort of mournful cosmic last resort
Is really tough on a girl, and she was pretty.
Anyway, she watched him pace the room
And finger his watch-chain and seem to sweat a bit,
And then she said one or two unprintable things.
But you mustn't judge her by that. What I mean to say is,
She's really all right. I still see her once in a while
And she always treats me right. We have a drink
And I give her a good time, and perhaps it's a year
Before I see her again, but there she is,
Running to fat, but dependable as they come.
And sometimes I bring her a bottle of *Nuit d'Amour*.

* Reprinted from *The Hard Hours*. Copyright © 1960, 1967 by Anthony E. Hecht.
New York: Atheneum Publishers, 1967, by permission of the publisher. This poem
originally appeared in *The Transatlantic Review*.

Suggestions for Papers

Short papers

Does this poem make you feel "over-protected, "*à la* Norman Holland and Gale Carrithers, Jr.?

How devastating a satire of "Dover Beach" is "The Dover Bitch"?

Does MacLeish's poem follow Arnold's in spirit?

What sort of comments would Charles Dickens (or Robert Browning, or Tennyson, or Thackeray) make about "Dover Beach"?

Did any of the above actually comment on the poem?

Is this a Christian poem?

Matthew Arnold died in 1888, the year of T.S. Eliot's birth. In what ways does "Dover Beach" suggest the themes of "The Wasteland" and/or "The Hollow Men"?

The Introduction to this book frequently refers to "Dover Beach" as a poem of despair, while Krieger calls it tragic, and Holland says it is reassuring, and Cadbury says it is cheerful. Who is right?

Long papers

Critics frequently speak of "Dover Beach" as a modern poem. (See Culler and Krieger for examples.) In what ways is it modern? Despite its modernity, could "Dover Beach" have been written in the twentieth century?

Reread 11. 23-49 of Wordsworth's "Tintern Abbey" and Norman Holland's essay. In what ways does Wordsworth appear to be describing Arnold's poetic method and confirming Holland's analysis? How closely does this process fit Krieger's description of extorting "symbolic instruction from a natural scene"?

Knoepflmacher writes of Arnold inverting Wordsworth's experience and consequently finding himself "stranded" without faith in a vitalizing spirit of Nature. How does this essentially literary analysis of Arnold square with the psychological approaches found in Holland, Carrithers, and in parts of Morrison?

Krieger makes passing reference to Virginia Woolf in his discussion of the modern sense of time in "Dover Beach." He also writes of moving from a particular setting or landscape to a less particularized sense of human tragedy. Read Woolf's *To the Lighthouse* and write an essay on the ways in which her symbolic use of the ocean and shore scenery resembles Arnold's. (For example, what happens when Mrs. Ramsay begins to hear the surf?)

Read some of Arnold's *Essays in Criticism* (First Series)—perhaps "The Function of Criticism," the Preface, "Pagan and Medieval Religious Sentiment." What, beside the title page, suggests that the man who wrote "Dover Beach" also wrote these essays?

One of Holland's most challenging claims is that his approach to "Dover Beach" does not contradict, but rather unifies other, more literary readings of the poem. How does Holland's reading reconcile, say, Cadbury's sense of the poem as a progression to Promethean freedom and Krieger's sense of men tragically aware of time?

Probably the most challenging critical question about "Dover Beach" is, How does a poem which ranges from room and window, to sea, beach, religion, Sophocles, Thucydides, war, and love, become a unified object? After reading all these essays, most of which try to answer that question, write out your own account of the poem, drawing on the essays, but by no means limiting yourself to them.

Additional Readings

Arnold, Matthew. *The Complete Prose Works,* ed. R. H. Super. Ann Arbor: University of Michigan Press, 1960– . 6 vols.

_____. *The Letters of Matthew Arnold to Arthur Hugh Clough,* ed. H. F. Lowry. Oxford: Oxford University Press, 1932.

_____. *The Poems,* ed. Kenneth Allott. London: Longmans, Green, and Company, Ltd., 1965.

Brown, E. K. *Matthew Arnold: A Study in Conflict.* Chicago: University of Chicago Press, 1948.

Holland, N. H. *The Dynamics of Literary Response.* Oxford: Oxford University Press, 1968.

James, D. G. *Matthew Arnold and the Decline of English Romanticism.* Oxford: Clarendon Press, 1962.

Johnson, E. D. H. *The Alien Vision of Victorian Poetry.* Princeton: Princeton University Press, 1952.

Johnson, W. S. *The Voices of Matthew Arnold.* New Haven: Yale University Press, 1961.

Miller, J. H. *The Disappearance of God.* Cambridge, Mass.: Belknap Press, 1963.

Trilling, Lionel. *Matthew Arnold.* Second edition. New York: Columbia University Press, 1958.

General Instructions
for a Research Paper

If your instructor gives you any specific directions about the format
of your research paper that differ from the directions given here, you
are, of course, to follow his directions. Otherwise, you can observe these
directions with the confidence that they represent fairly standard
conventions.

A research paper represents a student's synthesis of his reading in a
number of primary and secondary works, with an indication, in footnotes, of the source of quotations used in the paper or of facts cited in
paraphrased material. A *primary* source is the text of a work as it issued
from the pen of the author or some document contemporary with the
work. The following, for instance, would be considered primary sources:
a manuscript copy of the work; first editions of the work and any
subsequent editions authorized by the writer; a modern scholarly
edition of the text; an author's comment about his work in letters,
memoirs, diaries, journals, or periodicals; published comments on the
work by the author's contemporaries. A *secondary* source would be
any interpretation, explication, or evaluation of the work printed,
usually several years after the author's death, in critical articles and
books, in literary histories, and in biographies of the author. In this
casebook, the text of the work, any variant versions of it, any commentary on the work by the author himself or his contemporaries may
be considered as primary sources; the editor's Introduction, the articles from journals, and the excerpts from books are to be considered
secondary sources. The paper that you eventually write will become
a secondary source.

Plagiarism

The cardinal sin in the academic community is plagiarism. The
rankest form of plagiarism is the verbatim reproduction of someone
else's words without any indication that the passage is a quotation. A
lesser but still serious form of plagiarism is to report, in your own

words, the fruits of someone else's research without acknowledging the source of your information or interpretation.

You can take this as an inflexible rule: every verbatim quotation in your paper must be either enclosed in quotation marks or single-spaced and inset from the left-hand margin and must be followed by a footnote number. Students who merely change a few words or phrases in a quotation and present the passage as their own work are still guilty of plagiarism. Passages of genuine paraphrase must be footnoted too if the information or idea or interpretation contained in the paraphrase cannot be presumed to be known by ordinary educated people or at least by readers who would be interested in the subject you are writing about.

The penalties for plagiarism are usually very severe. Don't run the risk of a failing grade on the paper or even of a failing grade in the course.

Lead-Ins

Provide a lead-in for all quotations. Failure to do so results in a serious breakdown in coherence. The lead-in should at least name the person who is being quoted. The ideal lead-in, however, is one that not only names the person but indicates the pertinence of the quotation.

Examples:

> (typical lead-in for a single-spaced, inset quotation)

> Irving Babbitt makes this observation about Flaubert's attitude toward women:

(typical lead-in for quotation worked into the frame of one's sentence)

> Thus the poet sets out to show how the present age, as George Anderson puts it, "negates the values of the earlier revolution."[7]

Full Names

The first time you mention anyone in a paper give the full name of the person. Subsequently you may refer to him by his last name.

Examples: First allusion—Ronald S. Crane

Subsequent allusions—Professor Crane, as Crane says.

Ellipses

Lacunae in a direct quotation are indicated with *three spaced periods,* in addition to whatever punctuation mark was in the text at the point where you truncated the quotation. *Hit the space-bar of your type-writer between each period.* Usually there is no need to put the ellipsis-periods at the beginning or the end of a quotation.

Example: "The poets were not striving to communicate with their audience; . . . By and
large, the Romantics were seeking . . .
to express their unique personalities."[8]

Brackets

Brackets are used to enclose any material interpolated into a direct quotation. The abbreviation *sic,* enclosed in brackets, indicates that the error of spelling, grammar, or fact in a direct quotation has been copied as it was in the source being quoted. If your typewriter does not have special keys for brackets, draw the brackets neatly with a pen.

Examples: "He [Theodore Baum] maintained that Con-
fucianism [the primary element in Chinese
philosophy] aimed at teaching each individual to accept his lot in life."[12]

"Paul Revear [sic] made his historic ride
on April 18, 1875 [sic]."[15]

Summary Footnote

A footnote number at the end of a sentence which is not enclosed in quotation marks indicates that only *that* sentence is being docu-mented in the footnote. If you want to indicate that the footnote documents more than one sentence, put a footnote number at the end of the *first* sentence of the paraphrased passage and use some formula like this in the footnote:

[16] For the information presented in this and the
following paragraph, I am indebted to Marvin
Magalaner, Time of Apprenticeship: the Fiction of
Young James Joyce (London, 1959), pp. 81-93.

Citing the Edition

The edition of the author's work being used in a paper should always be cited in the first footnote that documents a quotation from that work. You can obviate the need for subsequent footnotes to that edition by using some formula like this:

⁴ Nathaniel Hawthorne, "Young Goodman Brown," as printed in <u>Young Goodman Brown</u>, ed. Thomas E. Connolly, Charles E. Merrill Literary Casebooks (Columbus, Ohio, 1968), pp. 3-15. This edition will be used throughout the paper, and hereafter all quotations from this book will be documented with a page-number in parentheses at the end of the quotation.

Notetaking

Although all the material you use in your paper may be contained in this casebook, you will find it easier to organize your paper if you work from notes written on 3 x 5 or 4 x 6 cards. Besides, you should get practice in the kind of notetaking you will have to do for other term-papers, when you will have to work from books and articles in, or on loan from, the library.

An ideal note is a self-contained note—one which has all the information you would need if you used anything from that note in your paper. A note will be self-contained if it carries the following information:

(1) The information or quotation *accurately* copied.

(2) Some system for distinguishing direct quotation from paraphrase.

(3) All the bibliographical information necessary for documenting that note—full name of the author, title, volume number (if any), place of publication, publisher, publication date, page numbers.

(4) If a question covered more than one page in the source, the note-card should indicate which part of the quotation occurred on one page and which part occurred on the next page. The easiest way to do this is to put the next page number in parentheses after the last word on one page and before the first word on the next page.

In short, your note should be so complete that you would never have to go back to the original source to gather any piece of information about that note.

Footnote Forms

The footnote forms used here follow the conventions set forth in the *MLA Style Sheet,* Revised Edition, ed. William Riley Parker, which is now used by more than 100 journals and more than thirty university presses in the United States. Copies of this pamphlet can be purchased for fifty cents from your university bookstore or from the Modern Language Association, 62 Fifth Avenue, New York, New York 10011. If your teacher or your institution prescribes a modified form of this footnoting system, you should, of course, follow that system.

A primary footnote, the form used the first time a source is cited, supplies four pieces of information: (1) author's name, (2) title of the source, (3) publication information, (4) specific location in the source of the information or quotation. A secondary footnote is the shorthand form of documentation after the source has been cited in full the first time.

Your instructor may permit you to put all your footnotes on separate pages at the end of your paper. But he may want to give you practice in putting footnotes at the bottom of the page. Whether the footnotes are put at the end of the paper or at the bottom of the page, they should observe this format of spacing: (1) the first line of each footnote should be indented, usually the same number of spaces as your paragraph indentations; (2) all subsequent lines of the footnote should start at the lefthand margin; (3) there should be single-spacing within each footnote and double-spacing between each footnote.

Example:

[10] Ruth Wallerstein, <u>Richard Crashaw</u>: <u>A Study in Style and Poetic Development</u>, University of Wisconsin Studies in Language and Literature, No. 37 (Madison, 1935), p. 52.

Primary Footnotes

(The form to be used the *first* time a work is cited)

[1] Paull F. Baum, <u>Ten Studies in the Poetry of Matthew Arnold</u> (Durham, N.C., 1958), p. 37.

(book by a single author; p. is the abbreviation of *page*)

[2] René Wellek and Austin Warren, <u>Theory of Literature</u> (New York, 1949), pp. 106-7.

(book by two authors; pp. is the abbreviation of *pages*)

³ William Hickling Prescott, History of the Reign
of Philip the Second, King of Spain, ed. John Foster
Kirk (Philadelphia, 1871), II, 47.

(an edited work of more than one volume; *ed.* is the abbreviation
for "edited by"; note that whenever a volume number is cited, the
abbreviation p. or pp. is *not* used in front of the page number)

⁴ John Pick, ed., The Windhover (Columbus, Ohio,
1968), p. 4.

(form for quotation from an editor's Introduction—as, for instance,
in this casebook series; here *ed.* is the abbreviation for "editor")

⁵ A.S.P. Woodhouse, "Nature and Grace in The Faerie
Queen," in Elizabethan Poetry: Modern Essays in
Criticism, ed. Paul J. Alpers (New York, 1967),
pp. 346-7.

                    (chapter or article from an edited collection)

⁶ Morton D. Paley, "Tyger of Wrath," PMLA, LXXXI
(December, 1966), 544.

(an article from a periodical; note that because the volume number
is cited no p. or pp. precedes the page number; the titles of periodicals are often abbreviated in footnotes but are spelled out in the
Bibliography; here, for instance, *PMLA* is the abbreviation for
Publications of the Modern Language Association)

Secondary Footnotes

(Abbreviated footnote forms to be used after a work has been cited
once in full)

⁷ Baum, p. 45.

(abbreviated form for work cited in footnote #1; note that the
secondary footnote is indented the same number of spaces as the
first line of primary footnotes)

⁸ Wellek and Warren, pp. 239-40.

                    (abbreviated form for work cited in footnote #2)

⁹ Prescott, II, 239.

(abbreviated form for work cited in footnote #3; because this is
a multi-volume work, the volume number must be given in addition to the page number)

¹⁰ Ibid., p. 245.

(refers to the immediately preceding footnote—that is, to page
245 in the second volume of Prescott's history; *ibid.* is the abbre-

viation of the Latin adverb *ibidem* meaning "in the same place"; note that this abbreviation is italicized or underlined and that it is followed by a period, because it is an abbreviation)

[11] Ibid., III, 103.

(refers to the immediately preceding footnote—that is, to Prescott's work again; there must be added to *ibid.* only what changes from the preceding footnote; here the volume and page changed; note that there is no p. before 103, because a volume number was cited)

[12] Baum, pp. 47-50.

(refers to the same work cited in footnote #7 and ultimately to the work cited in full in footnote #1)

[13] Paley, p. 547.

(refers to the article cited in footnote #6)

[14] Rebecca P. Parkin, "Mythopoeic Activity in the Rape of the Lock," ELH, XXI (March, 1954), 32.

(since this article from the *Journal of English Literary History* has not been previously cited in full, it must be given in full here)

[15] Ibid., pp. 33-4.

(refers to Parkin's article in the immediately preceding footnote)

Bibliography Forms

Note carefully the differences in bibliography forms from footnote forms: (1) the last name of the author is given first, since bibliography items are arranged alphabetically according to the surname of the author (in the case of two or more authors of a work, only the name of the first author is reversed) ; (2) the first line of each bibliography item starts at the lefthand margin; subsequent lines are indented; (3) periods are used instead of commas, and parentheses do not enclose publication information; (4) the publisher is given in addition to the place of publication; (5) the first and last pages of articles and chapters are given; (6) most of the abbreviations used in footnotes are avoided in the Bibliography.

The items are arranged here alphabetically as they would appear in the Bibliography of your paper.

Baum, Paull F. Ten Studies in the Poetry of Matthew Arnold. Durham, N.C.: University of North Carolina Press, 1958.

Paley, Morton D. "Tyger of Wrath," Publications of
    the Modern Language Association, LXXXI (Decem-
    ber, 1966), 540-51.

Parkin, Rebecca P. "Mythopoeic Activity in the Rape
    of the Lock," Journal of English Literary
    History, XXI (March, 1954), 30-8.

Pick, John, editor. The Windhover. Columbus, Ohio:
    Charles E. Merrill Publishing Company, 1968.

Prescott, William Hickling. History of the Reign of
    Philip the Second, King of Spain. Edited by
    John Foster Kirk. 3 volumes. Philadelphia: J.B.
    Lippincott and Company, 1871.

Wellek, René and Austin Warren. Theory of Litera-
    ture. New York: Harcourt, Brace & World, Inc.,
    1949.

Woodhouse, A.S.P. "Nature and Grace in The Faerie
    Queene," in Elizabethan Poetry: Modern Essays in
    Criticism. Edited by Paul J. Alpers. New York:
    Oxford University Press, 1967, pp. 345-79.

*If the form for some work that you are using in your paper is not given
in these samples of footnote and bibliography entries, ask your instructor for advice as to the proper form.*